JAILED FOR FREEDOM

JAILED FOR FREEDOM

American Women Win the Vote

DORIS STEVENS

EDITED BY CAROL O'HARE

FOREWORD BY EDITH MAYO
SMITHSONIAN INSTITUTION

NEWSAGE PRESS

Jailed for Freedom:
American Women Win the Vote

Revised Text Copyright 1995 by Carol O'Hare
Introduction Copyright 1995 by Edith Mayo

Softcover ISBN 0-939165-25-2

Address Inquiries to:
    NewSage Press
    P.O. Box 607
    Troutdale, OR 97060

Edited from the original edition, *Jailed for Freedom,* by Doris Stevens, first published in 1920.

Designed by Laura Shaw
Printed in the United States
Cover Photo: "College Day" pickets in front of the White House, 1917. Courtesy of the Smithsonian Institution.

Distributed by Publishers Group West

Library of Congress Cataloging-in-Publication Data

Stevens, Doris, 1892-1963.
    Jailed for freedom : American women win the vote / Doris Stevens ; edited by Carol O'Hare ; introduction by Edith Mayo.
        p. cm.
    "Edited from the original edition, 'Jailed for Freedom,' by Doris Stevens, first published in 1920"—T.p. verso.
    Includes bibliographical references and index.
    ISBN 0-939165-25-2 : $12.95
    1. Women—Suffrage—United States. I. O'Hare, Carol. II. Title.
JK1901.S85 1995
324.6'23'0973—dc20   95-2522
                                                              CIP

TO ALICE PAUL

through whose brilliant and devoted leadership
the women of America have been able
to consummate with gladness and gallant courage
their long struggle for political liberty,
this book is affectionately
dedicated

*Alice Paul unfurling the suffrage banner from the balcony at the National Woman's
Party headquarters in Washington, D.C., 1920. (National Woman's Party)*

I DO PRAY, and that most earnestly and constantly, for some terrific shock to startle the women of the nation into a self-respect which will compel them to see the absolute degradation of their present position; which will compel them to break their yoke of bondage and give them faith in themselves; which will make them proclaim their allegiance to women first.... The fact is, women are in chains, and their servitude is all the more debasing because they do not realize it. Oh to compel them to see and feel and to give them the courage and the conscience to speak and act for their own freedom, though they face the scorn and contempt of all the world for doing it!

NO SELF-RESPECTING WOMAN should wish or work for the success of a party that ignores her sex.

—SUSAN B. ANTHONY, 1872 and 1894

Contents

ACKNOWLEDGMENTS

My thanks to Marion Odell who first introduced me to the original 1920 version of *Jailed for Freedom,* to Julie Bennett for her early support, to Nancy Cott for sharing her research, and to Leila Rupp for the biographical information on Doris Stevens. I am indebted to Maureen Michelson at NewSage Press, not only for her willingness to publish this book, but also for her tremendous enthusiasm for the project. Edith Mayo has my deep appreciation for her thoughtful introduction that greatly adds to our understanding of these historic events. Special thanks to Robert Cooney, the Educational Film Center, the National Woman's Party, and the Smithsonian Institution for their photo research and assistance with photographs for the book.

And I am grateful to women everywhere, both past and present, whose efforts and dedication have helped ensure that all women will have freedom and political power.

—CAROL O'HARE

PREFACE

Jailed for Freedom tells the thrilling and memorable story of the militant suffragists' fight for the right to vote. In its original 1920 version, however, much of the drama was lost to modern-day readers in a sea of minute detail of legislative politics, author bias, and verbiage. It has been my goal in editing this new edition to bring this exciting story to life for today's audiences so that we may have a better understanding of the bitter struggle behind winning the vote. To this end, I have edited out sections that seemed extraneous and modified text to achieve clarity. I also added biographical sketches and historic background to explain people and events and to offer the reader some historic overview in which this story takes place.

Through it all, I have tried to keep intact the integrity of the original work, both in tone and content. Married women were identified by their husbands' names and single women were referred to formally with "Miss." In the index, however, I have made a point to add the married women's own names. Also, the text still includes terms such as "colored" or "negress" for African Americans in order to reflect accurately the historic tone.

Jailed for Freedom is not just a period piece of women's history; it is a story of independent women who were willing to battle for rights we take for granted today. It is a story both to celebrate and ponder, "How long must women wait for liberty?"

—CAROL O'HARE

INTRODUCTION

"We were but a handful…" recalled Elizabeth Cady Stanton reminiscing about the supporters of woman suffrage at the 1848 Seneca Falls Convention, when the right to vote was women's most radical demand. Between this first convention advocating the rights of women, and the ratification of the Nineteenth Amendment guaranteeing women's right to vote in 1920, lay a long and arduous journey. Victory was never assured until the final moment.

In the intervening years, the drive for suffrage encompassed the lives of several generations of women. The suffragists survived a series of dramatic transformations that included: fifty years of educating the public to establish the legitimacy of woman suffrage; nearly twenty years of direct militant action to press their claim to the vote; the division of each generation into moderate and radical camps; and the creation of a distinct female political culture to promote "votes for women."

This seventy-fifth anniversary edition of *Jailed for Freedom* has rendered this originally somewhat arcane political treatise into a highly readable, and readily understandable story for the modern reader that details a dramatic chapter in American history. For today's audiences, it is a clear, concise version retaining in vivid detail the dramatic, sometimes chilling, events that continue to have an impact on women's lives today. It brings to us the verve and spirit of this extraordinary assemblage of women with the freshness of a contemporary newspaper account.

When *Jailed for Freedom* was first published in 1920, its purpose was primarily to tell the story of the National Woman's Party (NWP), not the history of suffrage. Author Doris Stevens, and fellow National Woman's Party member, Inez Haynes Irwin, who wrote another account, *Uphill With Banners Flying* (also known as *The Story of Alice Paul and the National Woman's Party*), never considered that the history of militant suffrage would be forgotten. But the NWP membership dwindled with the passage of time, and the mainstream women's movement activists far outnumbered them. The mostly male historians who wrote our textbook histories virtually discounted the suffrage movement. If suffrage history was included, it was as part of Progressive Era reform, considered something that men of wisdom "gave" to women or, at best, a victory won by Susan B. Anthony and Carrie Chapman Catt.

Until the early 1970s, when women's history became a legitimate academic pursuit and women began writing their own history, suffrage was barely mentioned in textbooks, let alone militant activism by suffragists. Even in contemporary times—outside the ranks of women historians and feminists—Alice Paul and the National Woman's Party are hardly known. Few know that it was women seeking the vote who *first* picketed the White House for a political cause, or faced jail, hunger strikes, and forced feedings. For that matter, few have knowledge of Catt and the National American Woman Suffrage Association (NAWSA), and the years of strategizing and education in their fight for the vote.

In 1923, Catt and Nettie Rogers Shuler wrote in *Woman Suffrage and Politics,* "Hundreds of women gave the accumulated possibilities of an entire lifetime, thousands gave years of their lives, hundreds of thousands gave constant interest and such aid as they could. It was a continuous, seemingly endless, chain of activity. Young suffragists who helped forge the last links of that chain were not born when it began. Old suffragists who forged the first links were dead when it ended. It is doubtful if any man, even among suffrage men, ever realized what the suffrage struggle came to mean to women before the end was allowed in America."

The prevailing view of suffrage, when it appeared, was a version that envisioned a small, dogged, determined group of women who persisted against the odds until men finally "gave" them the vote. Until the advent of modern women's history, the story of militant suffrage had been virtually suppressed. The re-printing of *Jailed for Freedom,* then, is a particularly welcome event.

As an introduction to that chapter in American history when women fought and won the right to vote, a basic background of woman's suffrage in the United States will lay the groundwork for the historic drama that unfolds in *Jailed for Freedom*.

SENECA FALLS CONVENTION, 1848

Elizabeth Cady Stanton and Quaker activist, Lucretia Mott, had called the convention at Seneca Falls out of their deep anger with male abolitionists and the patriarchal system they represented. In 1840, when Stanton and Mott attended the World's Anti-Slavery Convention in London, the predominantly male convention refused to seat any female delegates. Stanton and Mott, like other activist women in the United States, began to see similarities between their own circumscribed status and that of the slaves. The Seneca Falls Convention lit a fire among women determined to change their legal and political position. Conventions were held with regularity during the 1850s, but the bitterness and bloodshed of the Civil War brought a halt to these activities as many women turned their efforts to war and relief work.

Expecting that their patriotism, war efforts, and agitation against slavery would be rewarded after the Civil War, women were bitterly disappointed. They soon found that Congress and the public felt that this was "the Negro's hour," and were not about to jeopardize citizenship and voting rights for black men by adding something so outrageous as votes for women.

Men and women who had worked for abolition and women's rights, prior to the Civil War, formed the Equal Rights Association to renew this work, once the war had ended. They supported the Thirteenth, Fourteenth, and Fifteenth Amendments to the Constitution that abolished slavery, conferred citizenship on African Americans, and granted the right to vote to African American men. Women were conspicuously and constitutionally omitted, and the Equal Rights Association could not agree on a single strategy to achieve woman suffrage. By 1869, the association had split into separate, warring camps. Many male abolitionists and many women felt that the cause of newly freed blacks came first, and subordinated the cause for women's rights. Radicals, such as Stanton and Anthony, felt that establishing women's equal citizenship and voting rights was of paramount importance.

By 1870, two new organizations emerged from the wreckage of the Equal Rights Association: the National Woman Suffrage Association and the American Woman Suffrage Association. There were theoretical and policy differences, as well as differences in approach and style, that led to the formation of these two groups. The National Woman Suffrage Association, led by Elizabeth Cady Stanton and Susan B. Anthony, espoused a radical platform of sweeping social change to improve the status of women, and advocated a constitutional amendment to guarantee women's voting rights. The National did not have male officers and few male members, and the very name of its periodical, *The Revolution,* gave evidence of this radical approach to women's rights.

Lucy Stone, a pioneer in abolition as well as women's rights, and Julia Ward Howe, a leader in the women's club movement (and author of the "Battle Hymn of the Republic"), along with several others, founded the more moderate American Woman Suffrage Association. This organization favored passage of woman suffrage voting laws at the state level. Their periodical, *The Woman's Journal,* had a polite, literary tone and did not stray far from "woman's sphere," although they did call for voting rights. Men were admitted to membership and even held leadership positions.

Both groups engaged in organizing and educational campaigns throughout the country. They gave speeches on the lecture circuit, distributed thousands of educational leaflets and pamphlets, and rallied support through presentations to women's clubs and temperance groups. These two women's rights associations waged relentless and grueling campaigns to support suffrage referenda in the states. However, the National Woman Suffrage Association also lobbied Congress. Year after year Anthony led deputations of women to urge passage of a constitutional amendment for woman suffrage. Despite all these efforts, Congressional hearings were rarely held, and the question of suffrage was sent to the floor for a vote only once, and failed.

By 1890, the fierce animosities of the previous generation of suffragists had abated, and a new cohort of women had joined the ranks.

The National and International Councils of Women, founded in 1888 at a convention attended by all factions and organizations within the women's movement, were enormously successful. Building on this success, the leaders in both the National and the American voted to unite to become the National American Woman Suffrage Association (NAWSA). This newly merged group took on the more moderate approach of the larger American Woman Suffrage Association; however, Stanton and Anthony remained leaders of the organization.

"Failure Is Impossible"

The pioneering work of Lucy Stone, combined with the intellectual and organizational partnership of Elizabeth Cady Stanton and Susan B. Anthony, dominated the drive for woman suffrage from the mid-nineteenth century until their deaths in 1893, 1902, and 1906, respectively. Despite their unflagging efforts and Anthony's rallying cry, "failure is impossible!" uttered at her last public appearance shortly before her death, success did not come in their lifetimes. At the turn of the century, only four Western states, Wyoming, Utah, Idaho, and Colorado, allowed women the right to vote. As the twentieth century began, the fifty-year-old suffrage movement, now represented by the NAWSA, was thoroughly mired in what its own leaders termed "the doldrums." Congressional hearings on a constitutional amendment for suffrage had not been held since 1887. Success was nowhere in sight.

Yet, the NAWSA and its predecessor organizations had sown the educational seeds of enfranchisement, ensuring abundant recruits for the new period of activism. By 1900, the movement's focus broadened and shifted from education to agitation, employing dramatic publicity, dynamic nonviolent confrontation, and civil disobedience to promote the cause.

A convergence of events also helped reinvigorate the movement. The Progressive Era (1890-1925) gave an impetus to all reform. Millions of women from all ethnic, class, and racial backgrounds entered public life to address severe social problems through innovative reform movements. As women's roles expanded in society, so did the political activism that politicized women and brought them into mainstream politics. Soon realizing that virtually every reform they sought was regulated by law, and that the legislators who passed these laws responded to voters, suffragists and women reformers alike believed that the social policy they supported could be achieved only if women had the vote. The question of woman suffrage had become mainstream politics.

New Suffrage Leaders

New leaders emerged whose brilliant organizational abilities and innovative tactical and political approaches revitalized the suffrage drive. One of these was Harriot Stanton Blatch, daughter of Elizabeth Cady Stanton. In 1902, she returned to New York after many years of living in England where she had witnessed the radical and innovative tactics and publicity generated by the militant British suffrage movement led by the Pankhurst women, Emmeline, Christabel, and Sylvia. Blatch was convinced that working women needed the vote to better their economic status, and that the suffrage movement needed working-class support. Like the Women's Trade Union League, she pioneered political alliances between middle-class and working-class suffrage supporters. Blatch set up a separate New York suffrage organization, the Equality League of Self-Supporting Women (later known as the Women's Political Union), introducing outdoor rallies, suffrage parades, and automobile tours that gained wide publicity for the cause and infused the American suffrage campaign with new life.

After Anthony's retirement in 1900, longtime organizer Carrie Chapman Catt assumed the leadership of the NAWSA. But only four years after emerging as the NAWSA's new leader, Catt was forced to leave office to care for her dying husband. Anna Howard Shaw, a close personal friend of Anthony's, became the NAWSA's leader. Although a veteran suffragist, a medical doctor, an ordained Methodist minister, and a powerful orator, Shaw was neither a strong leader nor an effective organizer. The NAWSA drifted.

Carrie Chapman Catt continued to pursue her commitment to suffrage once again after the death of her husband. With Shaw at the helm of NAWSA, Catt continued her suffrage work through other routes—as a founder and president of the International Woman Suffrage Alliance, and as the leader of the New York State suffrage campaign. She swiftly brought together most of the various New York City suffrage clubs under the banner of the Woman Suffrage Party. Catt organized New York City politically into wards and precincts to push for passage of woman suffrage. Her work was not sufficient to secure passage of the New York State suffrage referendum in 1915 against powerful vested interests, but Catt's extraordinary organizing abilities, powerful speaking style, and talent for fundraising brought her to the forefront of the movement again. (Suffrage passed in New York in 1917.) She returned to lead the NAWSA in 1915.

The third leader to emerge was Alice Paul, whose story we read in *Jailed for Freedom*. She, too, had been personally active in the British suffrage movement. Along with her militant British counterparts, Paul had been arrested and sent to jail where she went on hunger strikes and was force-fed while pressuring the government to grant woman suffrage.

The beginning of the Washington, D.C. parade, March 3, 1913. (National Woman's Party)

On returning to the United States, Paul recognized the need for intensive Congressional lobbying to secure votes for women. In late 1912, Paul persuaded the staid NAWSA, headquartered in New York, to permit her to organize a lobbying arm in Washington, D.C. Known as the Congressional Union, its sole purpose was to lobby for a federal woman suffrage amendment. It was agreed, and the NAWSA gave Paul exactly thirteen dollars for her annual lobbying budget!

Alice Paul gathered around her a group of women committed to the suffrage cause. She was determined to jolt Congress and the public into awareness through dramatic, public actions. The first public appearance of the Congressional Union was a suffrage spectacle unequalled in the political annals of the nation's capital. Paul and her strategists took advantage of the festive arrangements and publicity potential surrounding Woodrow Wilson's presidential inauguration in March, 1913. Paul planned a dramatic parade for the day preceding the Inaugural. The city was packed with party operatives and political well-wishers in the hundreds of thousands, most of whom lined Pennsylvania Avenue to watch the parade. Paul, a master of spectacle and street theater, coordinated a march of some 8,000 college women, professional women, working women, and middle-class members of the NAWSA into costumed marching units, each with its own banners.

Leading the parade in flowing white robes, astride a white horse, was the beautiful Inez Milholland (Boissevain). Suffrage floats and marching units followed down Pennsylvania Avenue from the Capitol past the White House. An elaborate suffrage tableau, then much in vogue, was to be held on the steps of the Treasury Building at the climax of the parade.

By the time this parade was staged, woman suffrage had gained political respectability among middle- and upper-class women. Paul counted many politically and socially well-connected women among her supporters. The general public and many male politicians, particularly in the East and the South, however, did not yet support votes for women. The predominantly male crowd watching the parade as it passed down Pennsylvania Avenue jeered, taunted, spat upon, and roughed up the women, disrupting the parade. Police did little to contain the unruly crowd or to protect the women. Fearing a riot, the

War Department called in mounted cavalry to restore order. It would prove an omen of things to come.

The mistreatment of many socially prominent women in the parade became an embarrassing debacle for the new Wilson Administration. Congress held hearings into police failure to protect a legitimate political parade, and the District of Columbia's Chief of Police, Richard Sylvester, was dismissed from his position.

Suddenly, however, the issue of suffrage—long thought dead by many politicians—was vividly alive in front-page headlines in newspapers across the country. The dramatic parade—and the ensuing scandal—had succeeded in capturing enormous publicity for the cause. Paul had accomplished her goal—to make woman suffrage a major political issue.

Alice Paul quickly followed this remarkable success with intensive lobbying campaigns. Congress, controlled by the Democratic Party with much of its stronghold in the conservative South, received the women lobbyists, but did little. Deputations of women to President Woodrow Wilson proved an exercise in futility.

By 1916, the suffrage drive experienced a major division that resulted in two primary suffragists' organization with very different tactics. As Paul intensified her lobbying efforts and escalated confrontational tactics, Catt took over the leadership of the NAWSA. In many ways opposites in political theory and style, Catt and Paul clashed over strategy. Paul's refusal to be limited in her politically confrontational tactics angered many moderate NAWSA members seeking respectable Congressional cooperation. Following the pattern established by the militant British suffrage women, Paul was determined to "hold the party in power responsible,"—the Democratic Party and President Wilson himself—for the failure to pass woman suffrage. On the other hand, Catt's tactic was to woo Wilson to the women's cause, not to enrage him, Congress, or the public by confrontational tactics. Catt feared that the cause would be stigmatized by violence, so she disavowed Paul's actions. A break was inevitable. The Congressional Union withdrew from the NAWSA and, in 1916, formed its own separate organization, the National Woman's Party (NWP), under Paul's leadership.

The political strategy of "holding the party in power responsible" for the failure to pass votes for women was a policy formulated by the militant Women's Social and Political Union in Britain. Held up by the NWP (as we learn in this work) and defended by many historians today, as a brilliant strategy, it had, in fact, far less application and effectiveness within the American political system with its three branches of government and system of "checks and balances" than it had under Britain's parliamentary system. Catt's "Winning Plan" strategy was far more closely tuned to the American system, combining the state-by-state approach that had been the traditional policy of the NAWSA with the realistic recognition that only a constitutional amendment would achieve women's right to vote.

When the author Doris Stevens and the NWP take credit for the increasingly successful lobbying efforts in the Congress, no mention is made of the critical fact that New York State, with its overwhelming number of Congressmen, approved suffrage in 1917, granting women the vote. The New York State victory was primarily the result of Catt's organizational work before she returned to the national leadership of the NAWSA.

"Holding the party in power responsible" also meant attacks on President Wilson personally as the leader of the Democratic Party. However, as *Jailed for Freedom* illustrates, the President was not always key to the party's actions. It demonstrates how party members from the South, a Democratic stronghold and home to many committee chairmen, were ultimately resistant to social change whether for African Americans or for women, and held up the Nineteenth Amendment even after Wilson's "enlightenment" and his vocal support.

What this strategy *did* provide was an organizing principle that guaranteed confrontation with the Democratic Party Congressional leadership, fostered debates over suffrage in the Western states where the NWP adherents sought to persuade women voters to cast their precious ballots against Democrats running for office, and insured embarrassment for President Wilson as he plunged the country into World War I to "make the world safe for democracy." In short, the policy led to dramatic nationwide publicity for woman suffrage, and highlighted the contradictions of denying women the right to vote while the nation fought for democracy.

As Paul led the NWP campaigns against Western Democrats in both the 1914 and 1916 elections, Catt announced her "Winning Plan" for woman suffrage. Catt, also a master organizer and political strategist, was able to breathe new life into state suffrage referenda by stressing to the NAWSA organizers that, once a state passed woman suffrage, its Congressmen and Senators would become de facto proponents for a federal suffrage amendment. Suffragists pursued state referenda across the country with renewed passion and vigor. As additional states passed voting rights for women, the number of suffrage supporters in the House and Senate increased, bringing the passage of a constitutional amendment nearer reality.

Carrie Chapman Catt also recognized the need for the NAWSA to have its own lobbyists in Congress to balance the militant approach of the NWP. In 1916, the NAWSA set up its own lobbying headquarters, "Suffrage House," in an impressive mansion on Rhode Island Avenue in Washington, D.C. Headed by Maud Wood Park, the NAWSA's lobbyists were collectively known by Congressmen as "The Front Door Lobby" because of their above-board political tactics, so unusual amidst the backroom dealings of the times. Both NAWSA and NWP lobbyists kept meticulous records on the life, family, personal preferences, idiosyncracies, and political record of each Congressman, and lobbied them relentlessly while in session to keep suffrage legislation moving ahead.

PICKETING THE WHITE HOUSE

Despite the relentless deputations to President Wilson, he refused to endorse suffrage. Startling the public and Congress, the NWP decided to dramatize their appeal by picketing the White House. They were the first group of citizens in American history to pioneer this form of political protest. In January 1917, the first suffrage pickets, known as "Silent Sentinels," appeared in front of the White House, holding banners with provocative political slogans or demanding the right to vote. In an atmosphere dominated by war hysteria and concerns for national unity in World War I, the women pickets were considered disloyal Americans by large segments of the public.

Unruly crowds often harassed the women, attacking them and destroying their banners. By June 1917, arrests of the women pickets began. While they had violated no law, and their picketing had always been peaceful, police arrested hundreds of women on trumped-up charges of "obstructing sidewalk traffic." In August 1917, a banner appeared decrying the hypocrisy of a President who himself was abroad advocating a policy to "make the world safe for democracy" while abridging civil liberties and suppressing self-determination at home. "Kaiser Wilson..." the banner began.

When the Woman's Party pickets came to trial, many, including Alice Paul, were convicted and sentenced to prison terms of up to six months in the District of Columbia Jail and the Occoquan Work-house in Virginia (now the location of the District of Columbia's correctional facility known as Lorton Prison). Paul and others demanded to be treated as political prisoners—imprisoned for their beliefs and not for any criminal act—and went on hunger strikes. The horrors of life at Occoquan, the brutality of the women's treatment at the hands of the guards and correctional officers, the "night of terror," and the torture of forced feedings, are graphically and grimly described in *Jailed for Freedom*. Paul was sent to the psychiatric ward where she was subjected to grueling interrogations by doctors from the District of Columbia's institution for the mentally insane, in an abortive effort to impugn her sanity and discredit her leadership of the suffrage movement.

The National Woman's Party members remained undaunted in the face of political repression and brutal treatment. In fact, it seemed to embolden them to escalate further their confrontational tactics. While many of their number continued to lobby Congress and the President, others persisted in picketing the White House, lighting suffrage "watchfires" in Lafayette Park and in front of the White House, and burning copies of the President's hypocritical speeches about democracy and self-government. At the same time, the NAWSA continued its pointed but nonconfrontational lobbying, and submitted petitions from state suffrage leagues.

As newspapers and magazines increased their reporting of the women's demand, public opinion began to turn in favor of the suffragists. Public and congressional outcry at the harsh treatment of the women escalated; respected public leaders demanded their release from jail. In an effort to end political embarrassment, the Administration ordered the women pardoned and released from prison. Ever the strategists, the NWP turned their members' jailing to their political advantage. Women released from jail, dressed in prison garb, garnered publicity by riding a train, called "The Prison Special," on a speaking tour throughout the country. Women also conducted automobile petition drives throughout the West and, as the vehicles made their way across the country, they stopped in cities and towns along the route where hundreds of thousands of women and men added their signatures to the suffrage petitions to be delivered to Congress.

Carrie Chapman Catt and the NAWSA disavowed Paul's tactics of "seditious" banners and "vulgar" demonstrations in favor of more traditional lobbying. The NAWSA, with nearly three million members by 1915, more nearly approximated culturally accepted female roles and was better able to bridge the gap between women's traditional roles and their new political role. The NWP, approximately 35,000 strong at its peak membership, embodied to many all that was feared in the changed roles implied by the "equality" of women.

Women's Political Culture

Creating a powerful political imagery was crucial in establishing a presence in the American public's consciousness and in bringing about the eventual acceptance of suffrage. As political parties evolved in the nineteenth century, and politicians and their supporters vied for the votes of an expanding popular electorate, male politicians created images of the soldier-statesman, the log-cabin common man, the rough-and-ready frontiersman, and the political sage, to achieve popular political support. In the late nineteenth century, as women expanded their roles outside the home into the public arena, they found no existing images in mainstream political culture that spoke to women's experiences or conveyed women's political objectives. It was *essen-*

The cover of the official program for the March 3, 1913 suffrage parade. (Smithsonian Institution)

tial that women create a powerful political culture of their own, including an iconography of suffrage—ideas converted into images— that would form a vital and instantly recognizable means of political communication in this pre-television age.

Out of the two distinct suffrage organizations, with their different philosophies and strategies, two separate suffrage imageries evolved. One set of images was aimed at mainstream women emphasizing "sainted" motherhood, "family values," and social service. The other was directed toward more radical women feminists and stressed equality, individual freedom, and personal empowerment. This powerful new political culture promoted women's inclusion in the public life of the nation, and proved a significant tactic that successfully helped to propel suffrage to final passage and ratification.

In creating a women's political culture, American women used materials rooted in indigenous traditions as well as others borrowed from the British suffrage movement and adapted to American usage. American suffrage women were inspired by parades, demonstrations, and symbols that drew on both British and American traditions in the political culture of the movement. The suffragists also embraced classical figures of women representing Liberty, Justice, Democracy, and America, which had been in political use since the time of the Revolution. The Woman's Christian Temperance Union had a history of street actions and public parades dating from the 1870s. California suffragists had staged parades as early as 1906 (prior to the first British suffrage parades) to promote a state amendment for women's vote.

Mainstream suffragists, represented by the NAWSA and its state affiliates, developed a powerful range of images promoting "Votes for Women," that stressed the nurturing and redemptive qualities of motherhood, social ministry, and social justice. Emphasizing women's role in the home, the nurturing and guardianship of children, and the building of communities, the NAWSA distributed a variety of propaganda—postcards, cartoons, fliers, buttons, and banners—that transformed women's role as homemakers and mothers into a compelling political rationale. "All matters pertaining to the home are women's business," was a frequently used slogan with images depicting respectable and competent women as guardians of the home and children.

Drawing parallels between housekeeping and politics, women extended their influence outward from the home into the public sphere, employing images promoting the protection of the home, and the "cleaning up" of "dirty politics," through "civic housekeeping." As Jane Addams, noted settlement house founder, social reformer, and peace advocate, announced in a *Ladies' Home Journal* article, "Politics is housekeeping on a grand scale."

The mainstream movement's emphasis on motherhood and the nurturing of children resulted in the use of culturally sanctioned images. This approach underscored the importance of women's uplifting role in society and promoted the production of idealized, Madonna-like poses of mother and child, echoing Christian imagery in support of the cause.

Color, a vivid symbol, was an instant means of visual communication in the suffrage movement. Several color themes were used by American suffrage groups: the indigenous American suffrage color of gold or yellow to connote light and the role of women as enlighteners; and the imported British suffrage colors purple, white, and green. Purple symbolized loyalty and dignity, white signified purity (also widely used in the American temperance movement), and green meant hope. Groups in New York, New Jersey, and Connecticut, influenced by Harriot Stanton Blatch's organization, used the British suffrage color combination of purple, white, and green. The National Woman's Party coupled the British purple and white with the use of the American color, gold.

Gold or yellow first came into use in the American movement in the much-publicized Kansas state suffrage campaign in 1867, in which the Kansas state symbol, the sunflower, was chosen as a suffrage symbol. The color gold was later used in suffrage songs to symbolize "the flame of freedom's fires." Coupled with a sunburst, the sun's rays, or a torch, gold signified the "dawn of a new day" for women. Thousands of gold banners, buttons, posters, and sashes emblazoned with suffrage slogans were used to promote "Votes for Women."

Both NAWSA moderates and NWP radicals used the herald as a symbol. This female figure, shown variously as an angelic figure with wings, or as a woman blowing a trumpet, holding a sword, riding a horse, or carrying a torch, was based on a figure created by Sylvia Pankhurst for the British movement. For general American audiences, these heralds were reminiscent of the goddesses of Liberty and Justice. Suffrage heralds were often coupled with sunbursts or rays of sunlight heralding a new day.

A variant on the use of the color gold and the herald was the figure of the "enlightened woman," a favorite suffrage image of both moderates and radicals. The NAWSA frequently circulated a map entitled "The Awakening," showing states in the West where women could vote. This image pictured a woman in classical robes, holding a torch, striding from West (where women could vote in some states) to East spreading the enlightenment of woman suffrage, as unenfranchised women in the East lifted their arms to reach for the torch. "Enlightenment" fit the American concept of woman's role as preserver and transmitter of culture, and was used as a symbol by both moderates and radicals. The NAWSA used the enlightening woman in its propaganda and tableaux. The Woman's Party adopted as its official motto, "Forward Out of Darkness, Forward Into Light," and often used banners with this slogan in parades and picketing.

While moderates and radicals shared some common American thematic elements, as well as the color gold, the NWP imagery was more militant in keeping with the philosophy of the Party. Inez Milholland (Boissevain) represents a classic study in the divergent imagery of the NAWSA and the NWP, as well as a transmutation of British suffrage imagery into American usage.

Inez Milholland's participation in two major suffrage parades, one in New York City in 1912, the other in the Washington, D.C. parade in March 1913, fixed her firmly in American suffrage imagery as the breathtaking figure of the herald. She is remembered by the descendants of the women's movement as "The Woman on a Horse." As the leader of both parades, Milholland had distinct cultural echoes of Joan of Arc, who had become the patron saint of the British suffrage movement. Militant, yet godly, the figure represented moral authority and suggested martyrdom for a righteous cause, both strong themes in the NWP's ideology. Joan, and by extension Inez Milholland as the herald, coupled woman's righteousness with divinely sanctioned, even divinely ordained, militancy. She symbolized the leadership of righteous women in a patriotic "Holy War," in a cause of self-sacrifice for God and country. The herald conveys at once unquestioned patriotism, and the redemption by godly women of venal and bumbling men for the good of the nation. Young women as well as life-long suffragists, moderates as well as militants, recognized her instantly.

In addition to portraying the herald, Milholland was also a lawyer and social activist whose true interest was reform causes. She enthusiastically worked long hours for the suffrage cause, to the point where, after several years of constant campaigning, her health began to suffer. Despite this, Milholland undertook a strenuous speaking tour in 1916 for the NWP to rally women in the enfranchised states of the West. While in Los Angeles speaking for suffrage and against President Wilson, Milholland collapsed while delivering a suffrage address. The last words ringing from her lips were: "Mr. President, how long must women wait for liberty?" With her death ten weeks later, the American woman suffrage movement lost a talented leader and its own martyr.

As *Jailed for Freedom* records, the memorial service for Milholland was a brilliantly staged pageant of suffrage symbolism. The NWP wasted no time in elevating her to sainthood and glorifying her death for the cause. On Christmas Day in 1916, Milholland was honored and eulogized in the first memorial service ever held for a woman in the U.S. Capitol. Suffragist Maude Younger of California delivered the memorial address, eulogizing Milholland as "...the flaming torch that went ahead to light the way—the symbol of light and freedom...."

After Milholland's death, the NWP circulated an idealized poster of her, a herald clad in flowing white robes, with gold helmet and star, riding a white horse and carrying a banner with the legend, "Forward Into Light." This classic poster became the official logo of the NWP that continues to the present, rendered in purple, on all official NWP correspondence.

Another militant image, that of a woman breaking free, emerging from her imprisoned role, was the "Jailed for Freedom" pin. With its representation of a prison gate secured with a heart-shaped lock, this pin was presented to all members of the NWP who served prison sentences for picketing the White House on behalf of suffrage. The prison door symbol was modeled after Sylvia Pankhurst's Holloway Brooch, representing the portcullis gate of Holloway Prison where British suffragists were incarcerated. The "Jailed for Freedom" pin was used exclusively by the NWP and suggests its origins in that militant group: a small cadre of committed, disciplined, militant women, set apart from mainstream suffragists, who were willing to go to prison for suffrage.

Suffrage Humor

Despite the sometimes heavily laden, often moralistic imagery, the suffrage movement was not without humor. Men had long used

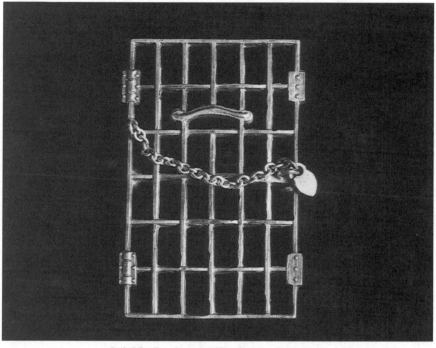

Jailed for Freedom pin. (Smithsonian Institution)

ridicule as a means of social control to keep women in their "proper sphere." Women now used comic postcards and cartoons to turn the tables on male opponents. Mainstream moderates stressed woman's redemptive role of "Sainted Motherhood" through social ministry, circulating postcards and graphics of a mother protecting her family and home from the evils of an all-male political system based on greed and corruption. Pro-suffrage cartoons emphasized woman's ability to "clean up politics." One cover page of *The Woman Citizen,* now the official organ of the NAWSA, pictured a woman using her political power to keep "booze," "vice," and "corrupt politics" from "the home."

Suffrage postcards favored by moderates often depicted children who could get away with communicating impertinent and assertive messages in a way that would have been socially unacceptable for their mothers to voice. One such postcard depicted a little boy trying to steal a kiss from a little girl who is holding him at arm's length and saying, "Suffrage First!" Another postcard featured a forlorn child who

Woman suffrage postcard. (Smithsonian Institution)

appeared to be lost in the woods. She carried a placard reading, "I Wish Mother Could Vote." Some mainstream postcards bore unmistakable adult humor, such as that which depicted a prominent gentleman who had come to listen to a street-corner suffrage speech, only to recognize—to his horror—that the speaker was his daughter! The caption, "And he thought she was just a little girl!"

Cartoons by Nina Allender were featured on the covers of the NWP publication, *The Suffragist*. These cartoons, in which adult women speak forthrightly for themselves, were often pointed, political barbs directed at the benighted male establishment represented by prominent politicians, Congress, and President Woodrow Wilson.

THE DUAL LEGACY OF SUFFRAGE

Such differences in imagery between the moderate NAWSA and the militant NWP are indicative not only of their differences in philosophy and style but embody their differing concepts of the nature of women.

While both the NAWSA and the NWP had diverse memberships, a variety of tactics and slogans, and adherents who espoused a variety of ideological stances, they had distinctly different approaches in acquiring woman's suffrage. The NWP was heir to the radical feminist tradition of the early National Woman Suffrage Association under the leadership of Stanton and Anthony. This ideology held that men and women were essentially equal except for differences in sexual biology. It stressed equality, individual freedom, and personal empowerment. In general, the more conservative NAWSA embodied the central ideological concept about the sexes in the nineteenth century—the "doctrine of separate spheres"—that held that men and women had fundamentally different natures, that women were morally superior to men, and that women's role was defined in terms of service to family, community, and state. Yet most women in both groups agreed that women's "special virtues" were needed outside their traditional sphere, especially in government and politics.

This dual legacy of suffrage has helped to complicate and divide the contemporary women's movement. It first manifested itself in the way in which the two suffrage organizations chose to continue their work of empowering women politically after the vote was won: the NWP was determined to introduce the Equal Rights Amendment (ERA), demanding complete equality under the law for women; and the NAWSA became the League of Women Voters, promoting informed citizenship, voter education and registration, and further women's service to community and state. The introduction of the ERA by the NWP in 1923 tore the women's movement apart for the next forty years, until passage of the Civil Rights Act of 1964. This Act assured working women, labor unions, and mainstream women's organizations that hard-won protective laws, which moderate women had struggled to enact for several generations, would not be abolished but, instead, extended to men and women on equal terms.

The dualistic imagery further heightened the division. Militant segments of the modern women's movement inherited the feminist aspects of the NWP and adopted essentially counter-cultural imagery, using strike fists and emphasizing self-actualization and individuality in promoting the ERA. For many mainstream women in the 1970s and 1980s, however, this imagery seemed harsh, radical, and unrelated to their lives. Yet, the politicized imagery of motherhood and self-less service set boundaries for women's political participation that continue to the present, "acceptable" boundaries beyond which women should not venture. The contemporary women's movement has yet to resolve either the conflicting imagery or the underlying philosophical differences that were so dramatically played out on the march to suffrage.

Rewriting History

Doris Stevens's *Jailed for Freedom* was not the first account of the suffrage movement to appear. The six-volume *History of Woman Suffrage,* begun in the late nineteenth century by suffragists Stanton, Anthony, and Matilda Joslyn Gage, was completed by author and NAWSA publicity head, Ida Husted Harper, at the time suffrage passed in 1920. Each work was an intensely partisan account of the suffrage movement. Neither Stevens's nor Harper's history mentioned or acknowledged the enormous contribution to the passage of the Nineteenth Amendment made by the other organization.

When the history of suffrage began to be written by contemporary women historians, they usually examined one group or the other, separately. Scholars began to write about the NWP because it offered a fertile, and largely unplowed field in women's history. In addition, during the 1970's the NWP's papers were finally deposited in the Library of Congress and made available on microfilm soon thereafter, opening a vast wealth of primary materials. Further, the militant tactics and the feminist ideology of the NWP more nearly approximated those used by the modern women's movement, a fact that made the NWP's story all the more interesting and relevant to modern scholars and activists alike. Only recently have historians produced suffrage studies that interweave the history of both the NAWSA and the NWP. A composite history is sorely needed to give a complete and accurate record of the events.

As for *Jailed for Freedom,* it gives us a dramatic, firsthand account of militant suffragists and their fight for the Nineteenth Amendment. This story reveals the real genius of the NWP. Its brilliant use of existing pre-television communications media was a precursor of the similarly inspired and innovative use of the mass media by the Civil Rights movement of the mid-1950s through much of the 1960s. Alice Paul's careful orchestration of deputations to the President, often by different groups of organized women (workers, college students, social settlement leaders, government employees, socially and politically well-connected women) was calculated to keep Wilson off balance so that he never knew quite what to expect. This created the forceful impression of a highly organized, well-educated, responsible battalion of women who wanted to vote, and were willing to be jailed for this right, and was a powerful force in the suffrage victory.

The NWP parades and demonstrations, too, were carefully planned to surprise, educate, and engage the public and the press. Paul created a series of themes and special events, and each action had a particular objective. As political theater, they were never repetitive, boring, or predictable. Paul and her fellow prisoners' determination to press the legal demand that the demonstrators be treated as political prisoners, their use of the hunger strike, and their endurance of force feeding continue to reverberate through twentieth century political protest.

Doris Stevens frequently describes the spirit of youth, the emotional freedom, the energy, and the sense of empowerment that invigorated one's soul when women stopped pleading for and began demanding their rights. This spirit can be summed up by one of the National Woman's Party's own suffrage banners that read: "Standing Together Women Shall Take Their Lives Into Their Own Keeping."

May we take the courageous legacy of these suffragists as our inspiration to face the ongoing challenges for full woman's equality in the twenty-first century.

—EDITH MAYO
Curator of Political History
Smithsonian Institution

CHAPTER ONE

Women Invade the Capitol

THE STREETS were nearly deserted when Woodrow Wilson arrived in Washington, D.C. It was March 3, 1913, the day before his first inauguration to the presidency. "Where are the people?" he asked. He had expected to be greeted at the station by a large crowd of supporters.

"On the avenue watching the suffragists parade," came the reply.

The people were indeed on Pennsylvania Avenue watching the suffragists parade. But this was no ordinary demonstration. Washington had never seen anything like it. Led by a young woman in flowing white robes on horseback, eight thousand women in costumed marching units—each with its own colorful banners—marched towards the White House. They were accompanied by marching bands and suffragists floats. Such a spectacle was unequaled in the nation's capital. It dramatized the fact that women wanted to vote and wanted an amendment to the Constitution of the United States giving them that right.

The march that day brought suffrage to the attention of the country in a way that could not have been anticipated nor planned. The huge crowd of spectators, in town for the inauguration festivities, became unruly and turned into a mob. Men threw insults at the women, physically attacked them, blocked their way, and all but broke up the beautiful spectacle. Although the women had been given a permit to march, the police stood by and did little to protect them. The march turned into a riot that was only brought under control by troops of calvary.

One Baltimore newspaper described the scene:

> Eight thousand women, marching in the woman suffrage pageant today, practically fought their way foot by foot up Pennsylvania Avenue, through a surging throng that completely defied Washington police, swamped the marchers, and broke their procession into little companies. The women, trudging stoutly along under great difficulties, were able to complete their march only when troops of calvary from Fort Myers were rushed into Washington to take charge of Pennsylvania Avenue. No inauguration has ever produced such scenes, which in many instances amounted to nothing less than riots.

Across the nation people were shocked and outraged at the idea of thousands of women being manhandled by irresponsible crowds because of police indifference. The events of the day nearly overshadowed the inauguration. An investigation of the incident was demand-

Inez Milholland on horseback leading the woman suffrage parade, up Pennsylvania Avenue, March 3, 1913. (Library of Congress)

k Out Receipt

Public Library (Sheboygan)
459-3400
meadpl.org

ay, September 22, 2019 3:32:58 PM

: 9000768588
e: Jailed for freedom : American women
the vote
rial: Book
10/20/2019

: 9000904857
e: Women's suffrage
rial: Book
10/20/2019

] items: 2

just saved $35.79 by using your librar
ou have saved $35.79 this past year an
1.68 since Dec. 2016!

Public Library
N. 8th St.
oygan, WI 53081
459-3400

fees charged as follows:
0 per day/per item=$2.00 maximum

ed following a storm of protest. The police administration was exonerated, but the District Chief of Police was quietly removed from his job.

This grand pageant was the first demonstration under the leadership of Alice Paul, the new chairman of the Congressional Committee of the National American Woman Suffrage Association (NAWSA). It was also the beginning of Woodrow Wilson's liberal education. The woman's suffrage issue would be brought often to his attention from then on until his final surrender six years later.

Four days after that historical parade, Alice Paul organized the first deputation of women ever to appear before a president to enlist his support for the passage of the national suffrage amendment. When the women, led by Miss Paul, entered the White House office, they found five chairs arranged in a row with one chair in front, like a classroom. The President came in and took his seat at the head of the "class."

After politely listening to the women, President Wilson responded that he had no opinion on the subject of woman suffrage; that he had never given it any thought; and that above all it was his task to see that Congress concentrate on the issues of currency revision and tariff reform. He was somewhat taken aback when Miss Paul addressed him with this query, "But Mr. President, do you not understand that the Administration has no right to legislate for currency, tariff, and any other reform without first getting the consent of women to these reforms?"

Get the consent of women. It was evident that this idea had not occurred to him. "This subject will receive my most careful consideration," was President Wilson's first suffrage promise.

He was given time to consider, and then a second deputation went to him, and then a third, asking him to include the suffrage amendment in his message to the new Congress. And still he was obsessed with the paramount considerations of "tariff" and "currency." He flatly stated there would be no time to consider suffrage for women. But the women kept right on insisting that the liberty of half the American people was more important than tariff and currency.

A second mass demonstration in support of the federal suffrage amendment was held on April 7, 1913, the opening day of President Wilson's first session of Congress. This time women delegates representing every one of the 435 Congressional Districts in the country carried petitions signed by the people back home asking for the passage of the amendment. The delegates marched on Congress, where they received a warm welcome and presented their petitions. On that day the amendment, which bore the name of Susan B. Anthony who drafted it in 1875, was reintroduced into both houses of Congress. It stated:

> Section 1. The right of citizens of the United States to vote shall not be denied or abridged by any State on account of sex.
> Section 2. Congress shall have the power, by appropriate legislation, to enforce the provisions of this article.

It was about this time that the Congressional Committee formed the Congressional Union for Woman Suffrage, a national organization whose sole purpose was to secure an amendment to the Constitution enfranchising women, rather than working for suffrage through the states. The five women of the Congressional Committee became part of the Executive Committee of the new organization, which remained a member of NAWSA. It adopted the colors of purple, white and gold, which would soon be seen at every suffrage gathering.

The month of May saw large gatherings throughout the country in support of the amendment, with the direct result that in June 1913 the Senate Committee on Suffrage made the first favorable report in *twenty-one years*. The measure was now on the Senate calendar for action.

The Congressional Union was determined to keep pressure on the Senate and so organized a third great demonstration for the last of July to present to the Senate a monster petition signed by hundreds of thousands of citizens asking that body to pass the national suffrage amendment. Women from all parts of the nation mobilized just outside of Washington in the Maryland countryside where they were met with appropriate ceremonies by members of the Union and the Senate Woman Suffrage Committee. The delegation then motored in gaily decorated automobiles to the Capitol and went directly to the Senate, where the entire day was given over to suffrage discussion.

Twenty-two Senators spoke in favor of the amendment. Three spoke against it. For the first time in *twenty-six years* suffrage was debated in Congress. That day was historic.

Speeches? Yes. Greetings? Yes. Present petitions from their con-
stituencies. Gladly. Report it from the Senate Committee. They had to
concede that. But passage of the amendment. That was still beyond
their contemplation.

More pressure was necessary. An appeal to action went out to the
women voters, of whom there were then nearly four million in the
nine Western states where suffrage already existed. It was decided to
bring some of these women voters to Washington to make Congress
aware of their existence.

The Congressional Union invited the Council of Women Voters to
hold its convention in Washington so that Congress might learn this
simple lesson: women did vote; there were four million of them; they
had a voters' organization; they cared about the enfranchisement of all
American women; they wanted the Senate to act; suffrage was no
longer a moral problem; it could be made a practical political problem
with which men and parties would have to reckon. The delegates to
the convention resolved that its organization would concentrate its
efforts upon the support of the federal amendment.

Meanwhile, the President's "paramount issues" of tariff and currency had been disposed of. With a new Congress set to convene in
December, he was preparing another message, so a fourth delegation
went to him. This time seventy-three women from the President's
own home state of New Jersey urged him to include recommendation
of the suffrage resolution in his message to Congress. At this interview
the President allowed that he was interested in seeing the formation of
a special committee on suffrage in the House and told them, "Rest
assured that I will give it my earnest attention."

Expressing this interest was a small thing the President was doing
to be sure, but at least he was doing something. It was our task to press
on until all the maze of Congressional machinery had been used to
exhaustion. Then there would be nothing left for them to do but to
pass the amendment.

For the fourth time that year, the determination of women to
secure the passage of the amendment was demonstrated. In December, during the opening week of the new Congress, the annual convention of the National American Woman Suffrage Association was

held in Washington. Lucy Burns, vice chairman of the Congressional Union, was applauded to the echo by the whole convention when she said:

> The National American Woman Suffrage Association is assembled in Washington to ask the Democratic Party to enfranchise the women of America. Rarely in the history of the country has a party been more powerful than the Democratic Party is today. It controls the Executive Office, the Senate and more than two-thirds of the members of the House of Representatives. It is in a position to give us effective and immediate help.
>
> We ask the Democrats to take action now. Inaction establishes just as clear a record as does a policy of open hostility.
>
> We have in our hands today not only the weapon of a just cause; we have the support of ten enfranchised states—states comprising one-fifth of the United States Senate, one seventh of the House of Representatives, and one-sixth of the electoral vote. More than 3,600,000 women have a vote in Presidential elections. It is unthinkable that a national government which represents women should ignore the issue of the right of all women to political freedom.
>
> We cannot wait until after the passage of scheduled Administration reforms. Congress is free to take action on our questions in the present session. We ask the Administration to support the woman suffrage amendment in Congress with its whole strength.

It was difficult to make the Administration believe that the women meant what they said, and that they meant to use every resource in their power, including militant action, to see it carried out. Men were used to having women ask them for suffrage. But they were disconcerted at being asked for it now and at being threatened with political chastisement if they did not yield to the demand.

In spite of the repeated requests to President Wilson that he include support of the measure in his speech to Congress, he failed to make any mention of the suffrage amendment when he delivered his message December 2.

The convention still in session, Miss Paul immediately organized it into a fifth deputation. A committee composed of representatives from each state went to the President to protest and to urge support of the amendment in a subsequent message. Dr. Anna Howard Shaw, president of the NAWSA, led the interview. In reply to her eloquent appeal for his assistance, the President said, "I am merely the spokesman of my party.... I have to confine myself to those things which have been embodied as promises to the people at an election."

I shall never forget that day. Shafts of sunlight came in at the window and fell full and square upon the white-haired leader who was in the closing days of her power. Her clear, deep, resonant voice, ringing with the genuine love of liberty, was in sharp contrast to the halting, timid, little and technical answer of the President. He stooped to utter some light pleasantry which he thought would no doubt please the "ladies." It did not provoke even a faint smile. Dr. Shaw had dramatically asked, "Mr. President, if *you* cannot speak for us and your party will not, who then, pray, is there to speak for us?"

"You seem very well able to speak for yourselves, ladies," with a broad smile, followed by a quick embarrassment when no one stirred.

"We mean, Mr. President, who will speak for us with *authority?*" came back the hot retort from Dr. Shaw.

The President made no reply. Instead he expressed a desire to shake the hands of the three hundred delegates. A few felt that manners compelled them to acquiesce; others filed out without this little political ceremony.

At the beginning of 1913 working with Congress on the amendment had seemed hopeless. But at the close of the year, despite the lack of presidential support, it had become a practical political issue. Alice Paul's report to the national convention for her year's work as chairman of the Congressional Committee of the NAWSA, and as chairman also of the Congressional Union for Woman Suffrage, showed that a budget of $27,000 had been raised and expended on Congressional work under her leadership as against *$10* spent during the previous year. Suffrage had entered the national field to stay.

At this point the Congressional Union resigned from the NAWSA and became an independent body. The main area of disagreement was that the Union wanted all suffrage work to focus on pressuring Congress and the President for a federal amendment. It also wanted to pursue a more vigorous, militant policy than the conservative suffrage leaders of NAWSA were willing to follow.

Hearings, deputations to the President, petitions to Congress, more persistent lobbying, all these things continued during the following year with the result that a vote in the Senate was taken, the first vote on suffrage in the Senate since 1887. The vote stood 36 to 34, thereby failing by 11 votes of the necessary two-thirds majority. This vote, nevertheless, indicated that a new strength in the suffrage battle had forced Congress to take some action.

In the House, the Rules Committee on a vote of 4 to 4 refused to create a suffrage committee. We appealed to the Democratic caucus to see if the party sustained this action. We wished to establish their party responsibility, one way or another. By a vote of 123 to 57 the caucus declared that "the question of woman suffrage is a state and not a federal question," and refused to create a committee on woman suffrage. This left no doubt as to how the Democratic Party stood.

Meanwhile the President had said to a deputation of working women who waited upon him in February, "Until the party, as such, has considered a matter of this very supreme importance, and taken its position, I am not at liberty to speak for it; and yet I am not at liberty to speak for it as an individual, for I am not an individual." To a delegation of five hundred club women he repeated his personal conviction that this was a matter for settlement by the states and not by the federal government.

It was necessary to appeal again to the nation. The Congressional Union called for demonstrations of public approval of the amendment in every state on May 2. Thousands of resolutions were passed calling for action in Congress. These resolutions were made the center of another great demonstration in Washington on May 9, 1914, when thousands of women in procession carried them to the steps of the Capitol. The resolutions were formally received by members of Congress and the demonstration ended dramatically with a great chorus of women massed on the steps singing "The March of the Women" to the thousands of spectators packed closely together on the Capitol grounds.

And still the President withheld his support.

Women had to face the fact that the Sixty-third Congress had made a distinctly hostile record on suffrage. The President, as leader of his party, had refused seven times all aid; the Democratic Party had recorded opposition through an adverse vote in the Senate and a caucus vote in the House forbidding consideration of the measure.

It became clear that some form of political action would have to be adopted which would prompt the Administration to act.

Anticipating the unfriendly record made by the Democrats in the Sixty-third Congress, Mrs. Oliver H. P. Belmont, one of the ablest suffrage leaders in the country, had met with Miss Paul and her vice chairman, Lucy Burns, to urge the formulation of a plan whereby we could strike at Administration opposition through the women voters of the West.

Mrs. Belmont was impatient to do nationally what she had already inaugurated in New York State—make suffrage an election issue. She was the first suffragist in America to be militant enough to wage a campaign against office seekers on the issue of woman suffrage. She had been associated with the Pankhursts in England and was the first suffrage leader here publicly to commend the tactics of the English militants. Through her, Mrs. Pankhurst made her first visits to America, where she found a sympathetic audience. But even among those who understood and believed in English tactics, it was thought that "militancy" would not be necessary in this country. In America, men would give women what women wanted without a struggle.

Mrs. Belmont was the one suffrage leader who foresaw that a militant battle here would be necessary to secure the vote for women, but she realized that political action would have to be exhausted first before attempting more aggressive tactics. And so, she urged Miss Paul to begin at once to organize the women's power for use in the approaching national Congressional election.

In August 1914 a program of action was submitted by Alice Paul and Lucy Burns with Mrs. Belmont's approval to the Congressional Union at a conference held at Marble House, Mrs. Belmont's Newport home. The plan stated that the dominant party, the Democratic Party, was responsible for all action on suffrage. Since that action had been hostile to this measure, the dominant party had to be convinced in the approaching election that opposition to suffrage was inexpedient.

An appeal would be made to the women voters in the nine suffrage states to withhold their support from the Democrats nationally, until the national Democratic Party ceased to block the suffrage amendment. All parties would thus be convinced to support suffrage when they saw that their opposition cost them votes. We would ask that women, as a disfranchised class, consider our right to vote preeminently over any other issue in any party's program.

Political leaders would resent our injecting our issue into their campaign, but the rank and file would only be won when they saw the loyalty of women to women. We knew this policy would be called militant and in a sense it was. It was strong, positive and energetic.

The plan was quickly adopted with tremendous enthusiasm by the conference and $7,000 pledged in a few moments to start it. And so, with resolute determination a tiny handful of women—never more than two, more often only one to a state—journeyed forth from Washington into the nine suffrage states of the West to put before the voting women this political plan and to ask them to support it.

CHAPTER TWO

Women Voters Organize

I T IS IMPOSSIBLE to give in a few words any adequate picture of the anger of Democratic leaders at our entrance into the campaign in the fall of 1914. Six weeks before election they woke up to find the issue of national suffrage injected into a campaign which they had meant should be no more stirring than an orderly and perfunctory endorsement of the President's legislative program.

The campaign became a very hot one during which most of the militancy seemed to be on the side of the political leaders. Heavy fists came down on desks. Harsh words were spoken. Violent threats were made. In Colorado, where I was campaigning, I was invited politely but firmly by the Democratic leader to leave the state the morning after I had arrived. "You can do no good here. I would advise you to leave at once. Besides, your plan is impracticable and the women will not support it."

"Then why do you object to my being here?" I asked.

"You have no right to ask women to do this…"

Every woman who took part in this campaign had similar experiences. The Democratic leaders did not welcome an issue raised unexpectedly, and one which forced them to spend an endless amount of time apologizing for and explaining their party's record.

This first entry of women into a national election on the suffrage amendment was little more than a quick, brilliant dash. With all its sketchiness, however, it had immediate political results. We had opposed all of the forty-three Democratic candidates running for Congress in the nine suffrage states, and only twenty were elected. While it was not our primary aim to defeat candidates, it was generally conceded that we had contributed to these defeats.

Our aim in this campaign was primarily to call to the attention of the public the bad suffrage record of the Democratic Party. The effect of our campaign was soon evident in Congress. Even the President perceived that the movement had gained new strength, though he was not yet politically moved by it. He was still tied to his conviction that suffrage ought to be brought about state by state.

During the year of 1914 the states of Nevada and Montana voted to give suffrage to women.

To show again in dramatic fashion the strength and will of the women voters to act on the suffrage issue, we made political work among the Western women the principal effort of the year 1915, the year preceding the presidential election. Taking advantage of the Panama-Pacific Exposition in San Francisco, we opened suffrage headquarters in the Palace of Education on the exposition grounds. From there we called the first Woman Voters' Convention ever held in the world for the single purpose of building political strength.

On September 14, 15 and 16, women from all the voting states assembled in a mass convention. These women from the deserts of Arizona, from the farms of Oregon, from the valleys of California, from the mountains of Nevada and Utah, were in deadly earnest. They had answered the call and they meant to stay in the fight until it was won. The convention went on record unanimously for further political action on behalf of national suffrage without compromise and pledged itself to use all power to this end without regard to the interests of any existing political party.

Two emissaries, Sara Bard Field and Frances Joliffe, both of California, were commissioned by women voters at the final session, when more than ten thousand people were present, to go to the President and Congress bearing these resolutions and a petition with hundreds of thousands of signatures gathered during the summer. They would speak directly to the President lest he should be inclined to take lightly the women voters' resolutions.

The envoys, symbolic of the new strength that was to come out of the West, made their journey across continent by automobile. They created a sensation all along the way, received as they were by governors, by mayors, by officials high and low, and by the populace. Thousands more added their names to the petition and it was rolled up to gigantic proportions until in December, when unrolled, it literally stretched over miles as it was borne to the Capitol with honor escorts.

When the women were mid-way across the continent, the President hastened to New Jersey to cast his vote for suffrage in a state referendum. He was careful to state that he did so as a private citizen, "not as the leader of my party in the nation." He repeated his opposition to national suffrage. "I believe it should be settled by the states and not by the national government, and that in no circumstances should it be made a party question; and my view has grown stronger at every turn of the agitation." The state amendment in New Jersey was certain to fail, as President Wilson well knew. Casting a vote for it would help his case with women voters and still not bring suffrage in the East a step nearer.

The Western envoys' reception at the Capitol was indeed dramatic. Thousands of women escorted them amid bands and banners and purple, gold and white pennants to the halls of Congress, where they were received by Senators and Representatives and addressed with eloquent speeches.

The envoys then met with the President at the White House. This visit of the representatives of women with power marked rather an advance in the President's position. He listened with an eager attention to the story of the new-found power and what women meant to do with it. For the first time on record, he said he had an open mind on the question of national suffrage and would confer with his party colleagues.

The Republican and Democratic National Committees heard the case of the envoys. They were also given a hearing before the Senate

Suffrage Committee and before the House Judiciary in one of the most lively and entertaining inquisitions in which women had ever participated.

No more questions on mother and home. No swan song for the passing of charm and womanly loveliness. Only agile scrambling by each committee member eager to ask, "If this amendment has not passed Congress by then, what will you do in the elections of 1916?" The women replied, "Sirs, that depends upon what you gentlemen do. We are asking a simple thing…" But they never got any further with their story, so eager was the Committee to jump ahead to political consequences.

"If President Wilson comes out for it and his party does not," from a Republican member, "will you…"

"I object to introducing partisan discussions here," interrupted a Democratic colleague. And so the hearing was something of a verbal riot, but there was no doubt as to the fact that Congressmen were alarmed by the prospect of women voting as a protest group.

In the new year, however, the problem of neutrality toward the European war was agitating the minds of political leaders. Nothing like suffrage for women must be allowed to rock the ship even slightly. It was men's business to keep the nation out of war, although men never had shown marked skill at keeping nations out of war in the history of the world.

The exciting national election contest of 1916 was approaching. Party conventions were scheduled to meet in June while the amendment languished at the Capitol. It was clear that more highly organized woman power would have to be called into action before the national government would speed its pace. The Eastern women once again went to the women voters of the West for decisive assistance.

A car known as the "Suffrage Special," carrying distinguished Eastern women and gifted speakers, made an extensive tour of the West and, under the tricolored banner of the Congressional Union, called upon the women voters to come to Chicago on June 5 to form a new party of women voters to serve as long as should be necessary as the balance of power in national contests, and thus to force action from the existing parties.

The instant response which met this appeal surprised the most optimistic hopes. Thousands of women assembled in Chicago for this convention, which became epoch-making not only in the suffrage fight but in the whole woman movement. For the first time in history, women came together to organize their political power into a party to free their own sex. For the first time in history representatives of men's political parties came to plead before these women voters for the support of their respective parties.

The convention resolved to form a new political party, The Woman's Party, composed of all Congressional Union members from the twelve suffrage states. It was a party with but one plank—the immediate passage of the federal suffrage amendment—a party determined to withhold its support from all existing parties until women were politically free, and to punish politically any party in power which did not use its power to free women; a party which would become a potent factor of protest in the following national election. Anne Martin, whose efforts had achieved suffrage in Nevada, was elected chairman.

This first step towards the solidarity of women quickly brought results. The Republican and Democratic National Conventions, meeting shortly after the convention, both included suffrage planks in their national platforms for the first time in history. To be sure, they were planks that failed to satisfy us, but the mere hint of organized political action on suffrage had moved the two dominant parties to advance a step.

The Republican platform was vague and indefinite on national suffrage, while the Democratic Party specifically recommended action by the individual states, not by Congress in a constitutional amendment. It was generally accepted that the President himself had written this suffrage plank.

Protected by the President's plank, the Democratic Congress continued to block national suffrage. It would not permit it even to be reported from the Judiciary Committee. The President, too, found it easy to hide behind the plank, claiming he could not act because the party plank, which he had written, prevented him from doing so!

Out of her frustration with the situation, Miss Mabel Vernon of Delaware became the first member of the Woman's Party to commit a "militant" act. President Wilson, speaking at the dedication of the Labor Temple in Washington, was declaring his interest in all classes and all struggles. He was proclaiming his beliefs in liberty and justice when Miss Vernon, who was seated on the platform near the President, said in her powerful voice, "Mr. President, if you sincerely desire to forward the interests of all the people, why do you oppose the national enfranchisement of women?" Despite their consternation, the members of the huge assembly realized women were protesting to the President against the denial of their liberty.

The President answered, "That is one of the things which we will have to take counsel over later," and resumed his speech. When Miss Vernon repeated her question later, she was ordered from the meeting by the police.

As the summer wore on, women realized that they would have to enter the national contest in the autumn to force action. The Woman's Party sought statements of the position on the national amendment from the two rival presidential candidates, Woodrow Wilson and Charles Evans Hughes, the Republican nominee.

Mr. Hughes, after a vigorous lobbying effort by Miss Paul, declared on August 1, 1916, "My view is that the proposed amendment should be submitted and ratified and the subject removed from political discussion." It was the first time any presidential candidate of either of the major political parties had publicly declared in favor of the federal amendment.

Meanwhile, the Democratic Congress adjourned without even reporting the measure for a vote and went forthwith to the country to ask reelection.

We also went to the country. We went to the women voters to lay before them again the Democratic Party's record. We asked women voters again to withhold their support nationally from President Wilson and his party.

Democratic speakers throughout the West were faced with an unexpected organized force among women who demanded an explanation of the past conduct of the Democratic Party and insisted on an immediate declaration by the President in favor of the amendment. They did their utmost to meet this opposition. "Give the President time. He can't do everything at once." "Trust him once more; he will do it for you next term." "He kept us out of war. He is the best friend the mothers of the nation ever had." "He stood by you. Now you women stand by him." "What good will votes do you if the Germans come over here and take your country?" And so on.

Although we entered this campaign with more strength than we had had in 1914, with a budget five times as large and with piled-up evidence of Democratic hostility, we could not have entered a more difficult contest. The people were excited to an almost unprecedented pitch over the issue of peace versus war in Europe. In spite of competing with this emotional situation, the issues of peace and suffrage were running almost neck and neck in the Western territory.

Practically every Democratic campaigner was forced to talk about suffrage. Some merely apologized and explained. Others spoke for the federal amendment and promised to work to put it through the next Congress, "if only you women will stand by Wilson and return him to power."

Space will not permit to give more than a hint of the scope and strength of our campaign. Women organizers went into all the Western states to prepare the way for a stream of speakers who attempted to convince, inform and inspire the women voters. Among the speakers were Harriot Stanton Blatch, daughter of pioneer suffragist Elizabeth Cady Stanton; Sara Bard Field, who had motored across the country carrying petitions from San Francisco; Maud Younger of California, a steadfast worker for the Congressional Union in Washington; and Rose Winslow, a Polish immigrant who represented women workers. Inez Milholland (Boissevain), who had led the March 3, 1913 parade in Washington, was appointed special flying envoy to make a swing through all the Western suffrage states, which now numbered twelve.

When Wilson campaigned with the slogan "He kept us out of war," the Woman's Party responded with "He kept us out of suffrage."

It must be made perfectly clear that the Woman's Party did not attempt to elect Mr. Hughes. The appeal was to cast a vote of protest against Mr. Wilson and his Congressional candidates, because he and his party had had the power to pass the amendment through Congress and refused to do so. That left the women free to choose from among the Republicans, Socialists and Prohibitionists.

History will never know how many women voted against the President and his party, for there were no records kept for men and women separately, except in Illinois. The women there voted two to one against Mr. Wilson and for Mr. Hughes. Men outnumbered women throughout the entire Western territory; in some states two or three to one. But, whereas, in the election of 1912, President Wilson got sixty-nine electoral votes from the suffrage states, in the 1916 election, when the whole West was aflame for him because of his peace policy, he received only fifty-seven. Our claim that the Democratic opposition to suffrage had cost votes was never seriously denied.

The Democratic Judiciary Committee of the House, which had refused to report suffrage for a vote, had only one Democratic member from a suffrage state, Mr. Joseph Taggart of Kansas, standing for reelection. This was the only spot where women could strike out against the action of this committee. They struck with success. He was defeated almost wholly by the women's votes.

With a modest campaign fund of slightly over $50,000, raised almost entirely in small sums, the women had forced the campaign committee of the Democratic Party to assume the defensive and practically to double expenditure and work on this issue. The Woman's Party protest was the only factor which stemmed the Western tide toward Wilson.

Again, with even more force, national suffrage had been injected into a campaign where it was not wanted, where the leaders had hoped the single issue of peace would hold the center of the stage. Again, many women had stood together on this issue and put woman suffrage first.

CHAPTER THREE

The Last Deputation to President Wilson

O F THE HUNDREDS of women who volunteered for the Western campaign, perhaps the most effective in their appeal were the disfranchised Eastern women.

The most dramatic figure of them all was Inez Milholland (Boissevain), the gallant and beloved crusader who gave her life that the day of women's freedom might be hastened. In the recent campaign she had traveled to eight states despite her own ill health, speaking day and night, frequently suffering from exhaustion. In September, as she was speaking at a mass meeting in Los Angeles, she fell fainting on the platform with the words, "Mr. President, how long must women wait for liberty?" Her fiery challenge was never heard again. She never recovered from the terrific strain of the campaign which had undermined her young strength, and in two months she was dead. Her death touched the heart of the nation; her sacrifice, made so generously for liberty, lighted anew the fire of rebellion in women, and aroused from inertia thousands never before interested in the liberation of their own sex.

Memorial meetings were held throughout the country at which women not only paid tribute to Inez Milholland, but reconsecrated themselves to the struggle and called again on the reelected President and his Congress to act.

The most impressive of these memorials was held on Christmas Day in Washington in Statuary Hall under the dome of the Capitol—the scene of memorial services for Lincoln and Garfield—filled with statues of outstanding figures in the struggle for political and religious liberty in this country. This was the first memorial service ever held in the Capitol to honor a woman.

Boy choristers led the procession singing the hymn,

> *Forward, out of error*
> *Leave behind the night*
> *Forward through the darkness*
> *Forward into light.*

They were followed into the hall by a procession of young girls dressed in purple, white and gold and bearing crusading banners high above their heads. There was music, tributes, resolutions, and an appeal to the Administration for action.

Maud Younger of California was chosen to make the memorial address. She said in part:

> We are here to pay tribute to Inez Milholland Boissevain, who was our comrade…. She stood for no man, no party. She stood only for woman….
>
> And as she had lived loving liberty, working for liberty, fighting for liberty, so it was that with this word on her lips she fell. "How long must women wait for liberty?" she cried and fell—as surely as any soldier upon the field of honor—as truly as any who ever gave up his life for an ideal.
>
> As in life she had been the symbol of the woman's cause so in death she is the symbol of its sacrifice. The whole daily sacrifice, the pouring out of life and strength that is the toll of woman's prolonged struggle.
>
> We are here today to pay tribute to Inez Milholland Boissevain…. Let our tribute be not words which pass, nor song which flies, nor flower which fades. Let it be this: that we finish the task she could not finish; that with new strength we take up the struggle in which fighting beside us she fell; that with new faith we consecrate ourselves to the cause of woman's freedom until

that cause is won; that with new devotion we go forth, inspired by her sacrifice, to...achieve full freedom for women, full democracy for the nation.

The women were in no mood merely to mourn the loss of a comrade-leader. The Government must be shown again its share of responsibility. Another appeal must be made to the President who, growing steadily in control over the people and over his Congress, was the one leader powerful enough to direct his party to accept this reform. But he was busy gathering his power to lead them elsewhere. Again we would have to compete with pro-war/anti-war sentiment. But it was no time to relax.

Following the holiday season a deputation of over three hundred women carried to the White House the Christmas Day memorial for Inez Milholland and other memorials from similar services. The President was brought face to face with the new protest of women against the continued waste of physical and spiritual energy in their battle.

The New York memorial read in part:

> This gathering appeals to you, the President of the United States, to end the outpouring of life and effort that has been made for the enfranchisement of women for more than seventy years in this country. The death of this lovely and brave woman symbolizes the whole daily sacrifice that vast numbers of women have made and are making for the sake of political freedom.
>
> We desire to make known to you, Mr. President, our deep sense of wrong being inflicted upon women in making them spend their health and strength and forcing them to abandon other work that means fuller self-expression, in order to win freedom under a government that professes to believe in democracy.
>
> We ask you with all the fervor and earnestness of our souls to exert your power over Congress in behalf of the national enfranchisement of women in the same way you have so successfully used it on other occasions and for far less important measures.

The serene and appealing voice of Sara Bard Field came as a temporary relief to the President—but only temporary. She brought tears to the eyes of the women as she said in presenting the California memorial resolutions:

> In the light of Inez Milholland's death, as we look over the long backward trail through which we have sought our political liberty, we are asking how long must this struggle go on.
>
> We have come here to you in the name of justice, in the name of democracy, in the name of all women who have fought and died for this cause. We have come asking you this day to speak some favorable word to us that we may know that you will use your good and great office to end this wasteful struggle of women.

The President responded:

> Ladies, I had not been apprised that you were coming here to make any representations that would issue an appeal to me. I had been told that you were coming to present memorial resolutions with regard to the very remarkable woman whom your cause has lost. I, therefore, am not prepared to say anything further than I have said on previous occasions of this sort.
>
> It is impossible for me, until the orders of my party are changed, to do anything other than I am doing as a party leader.
>
> In this country, as in every other self-governing country, it is really through the instrumentality of parties that things can be accomplished. They are not accomplished by the individual voice but by concerted action, and that action must come only so fast as you can concert it. I have done my best and continue to do my best in the interest of a cause in which I personally believe.

Dead silence. The President stood for a brief instant as if waiting for some faint stir of approval which did not come. He had the baffled air of a disappointed actor who has failed to reach his audience. Then he turned abruptly on his heel and left. Silently the women filed through the corridor and into the fresh air.

The women returned to their spacious Headquarters across the park all of one mind. How little the President knew about women. How he underestimated their intelligence and understanding of things political. How lightly had he shifted the responsibility for getting results to his party. Yet he and his party remained immovable. The three hundred women of the memorial deputation became on their return to Headquarters a spirited protest meeting.

Plans of action in the event the President refused to help had been under consideration by Alice Paul and her executive committee for some time, but they were now presented for the first time for approval. There was never a more dramatic moment at which to ask the women if they were ready for drastic action.

Harriot Stanton Blatch voiced the feeling of the entire body when she said, in a ringing call for action:

> We have gone to Congress, we have gone to the President during the last four years with great deputations, with small deputations. We have shown the interest all over the country in self-government for women. Yet he tells us today that it is up to us to convert his party. Why? Never before did the Democratic Party lie more in the hands of one man than it lies today in the hands of President Wilson. He controls his party, and I don't think he is too modest to know it. He can mold it as he wishes and yet he is not willing to lay a finger's weight on his party today for half the people of the United States.... He tells us that we must wait more—and more.
>
> We can't organize bigger and more influential deputations. We can't organize bigger processions. We can't, women, do anything more in that line. We have got to take a new departure. We have got to keep the question before him all the time. We have got to begin and begin immediately.
>
> Women, it rests with us. We have got to bring to the President, individually, day by day, week in and week out, the idea that great numbers of women want to be free, will be free, and want to know what he is going to do about it.
>
> Won't you come and join us in standing day after day at the gates of the White House with banners asking, "What will you do, Mr. President, for one-half the people of this nation?" Stand there as sentinels—sentinels of liberty, sentinels of self-government, silent sentinels. Let us stand beside the gateway where he

must pass in and out, so that he can never fail to realize that there is a tremendous earnestness and insistence back of this measure. Will you not show your allegiance today to this ideal of liberty? Will you not be a silent sentinel of liberty and self-government?

Deliberations continued. Details were quickly settled. Three thousand dollars was raised in a few minutes among these women, fresh from the President's rebuff. No one suggested waiting until the next presidential campaign. We could wait no longer. Volunteers signed up for sentinel duty and the fight was on.

CHAPTER FOUR

Picketing a President

O N JANUARY 10, 1917, the day following the memorial deputation to the President, the first line of sentinels, a dozen in number, appeared for duty at the White House gates. Eight of them carried purple, white and gold banners. Four women bore banners that
read:

MR. PRESIDENT, WHAT WILL YOU DO FOR WOMAN SUFFRAGE?

HOW LONG MUST WOMEN WAIT FOR LIBERTY?

It caused a profound stir and made the front page of all the newspapers in the country. Women carrying banners were standing quietly at
the White House gates picketing the President. Women wanted President Wilson to put his power behind the suffrage amendment in Congress. That did not seem so shocking and only a few editors condemned our actions.

When, however, the women went back on the picket line the next
day and the next and the next, it began to dawn upon the excited press
that such persistence was "undesirable"..."unwomanly"..."dangerous." Others picked up the refrain.

"Silly women"..."unsexed"..."pathological"..."They must be crazy"...
"Don't they know anything about politics?"..."What can Wilson do?
He does not have to sign the constitutional amendment." So ran the
comments from the wise elderly gentlemen sitting buried in cushioned
chairs at their club across the park, eagerly watching the "shocking,"
"shameless" women at the gates of the White House. No wonder these

gentlemen found the pickets irritating! Here were American women before their very eyes daring to shock them into thinking about liberty—liberty for women! This insult to the President could not go on. That women should stand at his gates asking for liberty was a sin without mitigation.

Disapproval of our picketing was not confined just to these gentlemen. I merely mention them as an example, for they were our neighbors. Yet, of course, we enjoyed irritating them. Knowing that our actions caused them such agony helped warm us while standing on the icy pavement on a damp day in the penetrating cold of a Washington winter.

There were faint rumblings also in Congress, but they were confined largely to the cloak rooms. One representative from Ohio did demand from the floor of the House that the "suffrage guard be withdrawn, as it is an insult to the President." Another named us "iron-jawed angels," and hoped we would soon retire. But these protests met with little response.

The Senate at that time was more interested in the prospect of our going into the European war. The beginning of our fight did indeed seem tiny and frail by the side of the big game of war, and so the Senators were at first scarcely aware that we were standing at the gates of the White House because the American Congress could not or would not act without being compelled to do so by the President.

The intrepid women stood their long vigils, day by day, at the White House gates, through biting wind and driving rain, through sleet and snow as well as sunshine, waiting for the President to act. Above all the challenges of their banners rang this simple, but insistent one:

MR. PRESIDENT, HOW LONG MUST WOMEN WAIT FOR LIBERTY?

The royal blaze of purple, white and gold—the Party's tricolored banners—made a gorgeous spot of color against the bare, black-limbed trees.

But there were no illusions in the hearts of the women who stood at their posts day in and day out. Their reactions were those of any human beings called upon to set their teeth doggedly and hang on to an unpleasant job. It seemed that anything but standing at a President's gate would be more diverting. But there we stood.

And what were the reflections of a President as he saw the indomitable little army at his gates? We can only venture to say, but at first he seemed amused and interested. Perhaps he thought it a trifling incident staged by a minority of the radical suffragists and anticipated no popular support for it. When he saw their persistence through a cruel winter his sympathy was touched. He ordered the guards to invite them in for a cup of hot coffee, which they declined. He raised his hat to them as he drove through the line. Sometimes he smiled. As yet he was not irritated. He was confident in his national power.

President Wilson passes the suffrage pickets in front of the White House, 1917. (National Woman's Party)

But with the country's entrance into the war and his immediate elevation to world leadership, the pickets began to be a serious thorn in his flesh. His own statements of faith in democracy and the necessity for establishing it throughout the world left him open to attack. The daily sight of the pickets, inspiring, gallant and impressive, escaped no one in the national capital. Distinguished visitors from the far corners of the earth passed by the women. Thousands read the compelling messages on the banners, and literally hundreds of thousands learned the story, when the visitors returned home.

Real displeasure over the sentinels by those who passed was negligible. There was some laughter and joking and an occasional sneer, but the vast majority were filled with admiration and encouragement. "Keep it up"…"You are on the right track"…"It is an outrage that you women should have to stand here and beg for your rights."

Often a lifted hat was held in sincere reverence over the heart as some courteous gentleman passed along the picket line. Of course there were some who came to try to argue with the pickets; who attempted to dissuade them from their persistent course. But the serene good humor and even temper of the women would not allow heated arguments to break in on the military precision of their line. If a question was asked, a picket would answer quietly.

A sweet old veteran of the Civil War said to one of my comrades, "Yous all right; you gotta fight for your rights in this world, and now that we are about to plunge into another war, I want to tell you women there'll be no end to it unless you women get power. We can't save ourselves and we need you. I am eighty-four years old, and I have watched this fight since I was a young man. Anything I can do to help, I want to do. I am living at the Old Soldier's Home and I ain't got much money, but here's something for your campaign. It's all I got, and God bless you, you've got to win." With that he shoved a crumpled two-dollar bill into her hand. His spirit made it an especially precious gift.

Cabinet members also passed and repassed. Congressmen by the hundreds came and went. Administration leaders tried to conceal their concern over our strategy with artificial indifference.

Women were coming from every state in the Union to take their place on the line. For the first time good "suffrage husbands" were made uncomfortable. Although they had always believed in suffrage and been uncomplaining when their wife's time was given to suffrage campaigning, it had not been enough. Now women were called upon for more intensive action and their husbands were not sure they approved.

It must be noted, however, that there were exceptional men of sensitive imaginations who supported women against their own hesitancy. They are the handful who gave women hope that they would not always have to struggle alone for their liberation.

Some women spectators, of course, did not approve of our actions, but more often we had their support. The more kind-hearted of them, inspired by the dauntless pickets standing in freezing temperatures, brought mittens, fur pieces, galoshes, hot bricks to stand on, raincoats, and coffee in thermos bottles.

Soon the pickets were the subject of animated conversation in practically every part of the nation. The press cartoonists, by their friendly and satirical comments, helped a great deal in popularizing the campaign. In spite of the bitter editorial comment of most of the press, the humor of the situation had an almost universal appeal.

People who had never before thought of suffrage for women had to think of it, if only to the extent of objecting to the way in which we asked for it. People who had thought a little about suffrage were compelled to think more about it. People who had believed in suffrage all their lives, but had never done a stroke of work for it, began to make speeches about it.

As soon as the regular picket line began to be accepted as a matter of course, we undertook to touch it up a bit to sustain public interest. State days were inaugurated, beginning with Maryland. There was a College Day, when women from fifteen American colleges stood on the line; a Teachers' Day, which found the long line represented by almost every state in the Union; and a Patriotic Day, when American flags mingled with the party's banners carried by members of the Women's Reserve Corps, Daughters of the Revolution and other patriotic organizations. And there were professional days when women doctors, lawyers and nurses joined the picket appeal. A huge labor demonstration brought women wage earners from offices and factories throughout the Eastern states.

A special Susan B. Anthony Day on February 15, the anniversary of the birth of that great pioneer, served to remind the President that women had been waiting and fighting for this legislation to pass Congress since the year 1878. In the face of heavy snow and rain, dozens of young women stood in line, holding special banners made for this occasion bearing her words, still as applicable today as when she first spoke them:

> WE PRESS OUR DEMAND FOR THE BALLOT AT THIS TIME IN
> NO NARROW, CAPTIOUS OR SELFISH SPIRIT, BUT FROM
> PUREST PATRIOTISM FOR THE HIGHEST GOOD OF EVERY
> CITIZEN, FOR THE SAFETY OF THE REPUBLIC AND AS A
> GLORIOUS EXAMPLE TO THE NATIONS OF THE EARTH.

President Wilson's second inauguration was rapidly approaching. Also, war clouds were gathering with all the increased emotionalism that comes at such a crisis. Some additional demonstration of power and force must be made before the President's inauguration and before the excitement of our entry into the war should plunge our cause into obscurity. This was the strategic moment to assemble our forces in convention in Washington.

Accordingly, the Congressional Union for Woman Suffrage and the Woman's Party, that section of the Congressional Union composed of women voters from the suffrage states, convened in Washington and decided unanimously to unite their strength, money and political power in one organization, to be called the National Woman's Party. Alice Paul was elected chairman.

Various resolutions were passed. It was decided to present these resolutions to the President on Inauguration Day with a dramatic picket line made up of one thousand delegates, and he was informed of our intent. The purpose was not only to carry to him the resolutions of the convention, but to plead with him to open his second administration with a promise to back the amendment.

In our optimism we hoped that this glorified picket-pageant might form a climax to our three months of picketing. The President admired persistence. He also said he appreciated the rare tenacity shown by our women. Surely now he would be convinced! The combined political strength of the Western women and the financial strength of the Eastern women would surely command his respect and entitle us to a hearing.

Inauguration Day, March 4, 1917, was a day of high wind and stinging, icy rain. A thousand women marched, each bearing a banner, struggling against the gale to keep their banners erect. They marched in rain-soaked garments, hands bare, gloves torn by the sticky varnish from the banner poles, and streams of water running down the poles into the palms of their hands. It was a sight to impress even the most hardened spectator who had seen all the various forms of the suffrage agitation in Washington. Long before the appointed hour for the march to start, thousands of spectators lined the streets to watch the procession. Two bands managed to continue their spirited music in spite of the driving rain.

Vida Milholland led the procession carrying a golden banner with her sister's last words:

MR. PRESIDENT, HOW LONG MUST WOMEN WAIT FOR LIBERTY?

Next came the Great Demand banner:

WE DEMAND AN AMENDMENT TO THE CONSTITUTION OF THE
UNITED STATES ENFRANCHISING WOMEN.

It was followed by the banner Inez Milholland had carried in her first suffrage procession in New York. The long line of women bearing the purple, white and gold fell in behind.

Most extraordinary precautions had been taken about the White House. There were almost as many police officers as marchers. On every fifty feet of curb around the entire White House grounds there was a policeman. On the inside of the tall picket fence which surrounds the grounds were as many more.

We proceeded to the main gate. Locked! A White House guard told us that he had orders to keep the gates locked. The procession continued on to the second gate on Pennsylvania Avenue. Again locked. "You can't come in here," stated a nervous policeman. The line made its way to the third and last gate—the gate leading to the Executive offices. We could see a small army of grinning clerks and secretaries at the windows, evidently amused at the sight of the women struggling in the wind and rain to keep their banners intact. The leaders stayed at this gate, determined to get results from the guard, while the rest of the women continued to circle the White House.

Finally the guard was convinced to take a message to the President's Secretary asking him to tell the President that we were waiting to see him. He had scarcely got inside when he rushed back to his post. When we sought to ascertain what had happened, he quietly confided to us that he had been reprimanded for leaving his post.

For more than two hours the women marched, circling the White House four times—the rain never ceasing for an instant, the cold almost unendurable—hoping to the last moment that at least their leaders would be allowed to take in to the President the resolutions which they were carrying.

The white-haired grandmothers in the procession—there were some as old as eighty-four—were as energetic as the young girls of twenty. Women marched and waited, waited and marched, under the sting of the biting elements and under the worse sting of the indignities heaped upon them. It was impossible to believe that in democratic America they could not see the President to lay before him their grievance.

It was only when they saw the presidential limousine, in the late afternoon, roll luxuriously out of the grounds and through the gates down Pennsylvania Avenue, that the weary marchers realized that President Wilson had deliberately turned them away unheard. The car, as it came through the gates, divided the banner-bearers. President and Mrs. Wilson looked straight ahead as if the long line of purple, white and gold was invisible.

All the women who took part in that march will tell you of the passionate resentment that burned in their hearts on that dreary day. This one single incident probably did more than any other to make women sacrifice themselves. Even something as thin as diplomacy on the part of President Wilson might have saved him many restless hours to follow, but he did not take the trouble to exercise even that.

Three months of picketing had not been enough. We must not only continue on duty at his gates but also at the gates of Congress.

CHAPTER FIVE

The Suffrage War Policy

PRESIDENT WILSON called the War Session of the Sixty-fifth Congress on April 2, 1917. (By this time nineteen States had granted women the right to vote.)

On the opening day of Congress not only were the pickets again on duty at the White House, but another picket line was inaugurated at the Capitol. Returning Senators and Congressmen were surprised when greeted with great golden banners reading:

RUSSIA AND ENGLAND ARE ENFRANCHISING THEIR WOMEN IN WAR-TIME. HOW LONG MUST AMERICAN WOMEN WAIT FOR THEIR LIBERTY?

The last desperate flurries in the pro-war and anti-war camps were focused on the Capitol that day. Pacifists from all over the country, wearing white badges, and advocates of war, wearing the national colors, swarmed about the grounds and through the buildings. Our sentinels stood strangely silent and almost aloof, strong in their dedication to democracy, while the peace and war agitation circled about them.

On April 7, Congress declared the United States to be at war with Germany. President Wilson voiced his memorable, "We shall fight for the things we have always carried nearest our hearts—for democracy—for the right of those who submit to authority to have a voice in their own Government." Inspiring words indeed!

Now that the United States was actually involved in war, we were face to face with the question, which we had considered at the convention the previous month, as to what position we, as an organization, should take in this situation.

The atmosphere of that convention had been dramatic. Most of the delegates had been urged to persuade the organization to abandon its work for the freedom of women and to turn its activities into war channels. Although war was then only rumored, a hysterical attitude was already prevalent. Women were asked to furl their banners and give up their half-century struggle for democracy, to forget the liberty that was most precious to their hearts.

"The President will turn this imperialist war into a crusade for democracy." "Lay aside your own fight and help us crush Germany, and you will find yourselves rewarded with a vote out of the nation's gratitude," were some of the appeals made to our women by government officials and the public. Despite these appeals and promises, never in history did a band of women stand together with more sanity and greater solidarity than did these thousand delegates representing thousands more throughout the States.

We had banded together to secure political freedom for women. We were united on no other subject. Some would offer passive resistance to the war; others would support a vigorous military policy. Between these, every shade of opinion was represented. Each was loyal to her own ideas which she held for her country. The National Woman's Party, we maintained, was concerned only with the effort to obtain political power for women, whatever their ideals.

The thousand delegates present at the convention, though differing widely on the duty of the individual in war, were unanimous in voting that in the event of war, the National Woman's Party, as an *organization,* should continue to work for political liberty for women and for that alone, believing that in so doing the organization served the highest interest of the country. The Woman's Party was created, according to its constitution, for one purpose only—"to secure an amendment to the United States Constitution enfranchising women."

Despite the fact that Europe, then approaching her third year of war, was increasing democracy in the midst of the terrible conflict, in America women were being told that no attempt at electoral reform had any place in the country's program until the war was over. The Democrats met in caucus and decided that only "war measures" should be included in the legislative program, and announced that no subjects would be considered by them, unless the President urged them as war measures.

Our task was, from that time on, to make national suffrage a war measure. We at once urged the Administration to accept our proposed reform as a war measure, and pointed out the difficulty of waging a war for democracy abroad while democracy was denied at home. But the Government was still resistant to extending suffrage to women.

We must confess that the problem of dramatizing our fight for democracy in competition with the drama of a world war was most perplexing. Here were we, citizens without power and recognition. We could not and would not fight with the weapons men use in the pursuit of democracy—bayonets, machine guns, poison gas, deadly grenades, bombs, armored tanks, pistols, barbed wire entanglements, submarines, and mines. What would we do? We would continue to fight with our simple, peaceful, almost quaint device—a banner.

Just as our political strategy at elections had been to oppose the party in power which had failed to use its power to free women, so now our military strategy was based on the military doctrine of concentrating all one's forces on the enemy's weakest point. For women, the weakest point in the Administration's political lines during the war was the inconsistency between a crusade for world democracy and the denial of democracy at home. This was the untenable position of President Wilson and the Democratic Administration, from which we must force them to retreat. We intended to expose this weakest point to the critical eyes of the world.

The President's sudden elevation to the powerful position of a world leader and the champion of democracy was at once an advantage and a disadvantage to us. It was an advantage to us in that it made our attack more dramatic. It was a disadvantage to have to overcome this universal trust and world-wide popularity. But this conflict of wits and brains against power only enhanced our ingenuity.

On the day the heads of the English and French missions visited the White House, our banners bore these inscriptions:

WE SHALL FIGHT FOR THE THINGS WE HAVE ALWAYS
HELD NEAREST OUR HEARTS.

DEMOCRACY SHOULD BEGIN AT HOME.

WE DEMAND JUSTICE AND SELF GOVERNMENT AT HOME.

Embarrassing to say these things before foreign visitors? We hoped it would be. Our only hope of success lay in our capacity to embarrass Mr. Wilson and his Administration. We had to keep before the country the flagrant inconsistency of the President's position. We intended to know why, if democracy were so precious as to demand the nation's blood for its achievement abroad, its execution at home was so undesirable.

Some rumblings of political action began to be heard. The Democratic majority had appointed a Senate Committee on Woman Suffrage whose members were overwhelmingly for federal action. Its chairman promised an early report. Representatives and Senators were tumbling over each other to introduce similar suffrage resolutions. We actually had difficulty in choosing the man whose name should stamp our measure.

A minority party also was moved to act. Members of the Progressive Party adopted a suffrage plank at their convention which demanded the nationwide enfranchisement of women. They also voted to send a committee consisting of representatives of all liberal groups to Washington to present to the President and Congress "a demand for immediate submission of an amendment to the United States Constitution enfranchising women."

The committee included representatives from the Progressive Party, the Socialist Party, the Prohibition Party, and the National Woman's Party. It was the first suffrage conference with the President after the declaration of war and was the last deputation on suffrage by minority party leaders.

The President was deeply moved when Mabel Vernon of the Woman's Party said:

> If the right of those who submit to authority to have a voice in their own government is so sacred a cause to foreign people as to constitute the reason for our entering the international war in its defense, will you not, Mr. President, give immediate aid to the measure before Congress demanding self-government for the women of this country?

The President admitted that suffrage was constantly upon his mind for reconsideration. He added, however, that the program for the session was practically complete and intimated that it did not include the enfranchisement of women. While he did inform the committee that he was in favor of the creation of a Woman Suffrage Committee in the House of Representatives, he could have just as easily have asked the Senate Committee on Suffrage or the Judiciary Committee of the House for an immediate report on the suffrage resolution rather than create another committee.

He made no mention of his state-by-state conviction, however, as he had in previous interviews, and it was understood that he at least tacitly accepted federal action. The House Judiciary continued to refuse to act and the House Rules Committee steadily refused to create a Suffrage Committee. But the Republicans, hoping to win back the Progressives who had demonstrated their allegiance to suffrage, and seeing an opportunity to embarrass the Administration, began to show interest in action on the amendment.

The Administration was aroused. It did not know how far the Republicans were prepared to go in their drive for action, and so the House Rules Committee suddenly met and its Democratic majority reported favorably on the resolution providing for a Woman Suffrage Committee in the House "after all pending war measures have been disposed of."

Still uncertain of the intent of the Republicans, the Democrats were moved to further action. A few days later the Executive Committee of the Democratic National Committee voted to "officially urge upon the President that he call the two Houses of Congress together and recommend the immediate submission of the Susan B. Anthony amendment." The Republicans' actions quickly subsided when they saw the Democrats making an advance. And so the Democratic Executive Committee now said that its act was not really official, but merely reflected the "personal conviction" of the members present. As a result, of course, no action followed in Congress.

And so it went—like a great game of chess. Doubtless the politicians believed they were moved from their own true and noble motives. The fact was that the pickets had moved the Democrats a step. The Republicans had then attempted to take two steps, where-upon the Democrats must continue to move more rapidly than their opponents. Behind this matching of political wits by the two parties stood the faithful pickets compelling them both to act.

Simultaneously with these moves and countermoves in political circles, the people in all sections of this vast country began to speak their minds. Meetings were springing up everywhere, at which resolutions were passed backing up the picket line and urging the President and Congress to act. Even the South, the Administration's stronghold, sent fiery telegrams demanding action. Alabama, South Carolina, Texas, Maryland, Mississippi, as well as the West, Middle West, New England and the East—the stream was endless.

Every time a new piece of legislation was passed—the war tax bill, food conservation or what not—women from unexpected quarters sent to the Government their protest against the passage of measures so vital to women without women's consent, coupled with an appeal for the liberation of women. Club women, college women, federations of labor, all kinds of organizations sent protests to the Administration leaders. The picket line, approaching its sixth month, had aroused the country to an unprecedented interest in suffrage; it had rallied widespread public support to the amendment as a war measure, and had itself become almost universally accepted if not universally approved. And in the midst of picketing and in spite of all the prophecies and fears that our actions would "set back the cause," within one month, Michigan, Nebraska and Rhode Island granted presidential suffrage to women.

The Administration leaders were busy marshaling their forces behind the President's war program, which included the controversial Conscription and Espionage Bills, then pending, and did not relish having our question so vivid in the public mind.

The manifestations of popular approval of suffrage, the constant stream of protests to the Administration against its delay nationally, and the shame of having women begging at its gates, could result in only one of two things. The Administration had little choice. It must yield to this pressure or it must suppress the agitation. It must pass the amendment or remove the troublesome pickets.

The Administration decided to remove the pickets.

Chapter Six

The First Arrests

T HE ADMINISTRATION chose suppression. They resorted to force in an attempt to end picketing. It was a policy doomed to failure as certainly as all resorts to force to kill agitation have ultimately failed. This marked the beginning of the adoption by the Administration of tactics from which they could never extricate themselves with honor. Unfortunately for them they were entering upon this policy toward women which savored of czarist practices, at the very moment they were congratulating the Russians upon their liberation from the oppression of a czar. This fact supplied us with a fresh angle of attack.

President Wilson had sent a mission to Russia to persuade that country to continue the war and to convince her people of its democratic purpose, and of the democratic quality of America. One of the President's envoys stated that he represented a republic where there was "universal, direct, equal and secret suffrage." We would subject the President to attack through this statement.

When Russia sent a war mission to our country for purposes of cooperation, the occasion offered us the opportunity again to expose the Administration's weakness in claiming complete political democracy while women were still denied their political freedom.

It was a beautiful June day when all Washington was agog with the visit of the Russian diplomats to the President. As the car carrying the envoys passed swiftly through the gates of the White House, there stood on the picket line two silent sentinels, Lucy Burns of New York and Mrs. Lawrence Lewis of Philadelphia, with a great lettered banner which read:

TO THE RUSSIAN ENVOYS, WE THE WOMEN OF AMERICA TELL YOU THAT AMERICA IS NOT A DEMOCRACY. TWENTY MILLION AMERICAN WOMEN ARE DENIED THE RIGHT TO VOTE. PRESIDENT WILSON IS THE CHIEF OPPONENT OF THEIR NATIONAL ENFRANCHISEMENT. HELP US MAKE THIS NATION REALLY FREE. TELL OUR GOVERNMENT IT MUST LIBERATE ITS PEOPLE BEFORE IT CAN CLAIM FREE RUSSIA AS AN ALLY.

Rumors that the suffragists would make a special demonstration before the Russian mission had brought a great crowd to the gate of the White House; a crowd composed almost entirely of men. Like all crowds, this one had its share of hoodlums and rowdies who tried to interfere with the women. As soon as the diplomats had passed, a man tore down our banner. The next day, June 21, a similar banner was destroyed by some boys while the police looked on. New banners brought from Headquarters were also torn down. Finally police reserves restored order and peaceful picketing resumed.

There was criticism in the press and on the lips of men that we were embarrassing our Government before the eyes of foreign visitors. In answering the criticism, Miss Paul publicly stated our position, "The intolerable conditions against which we protest can be changed in a twinkling of an eye. The responsibility for our protest is, therefore, with the Administration and not with the women of America, if the lack of democracy at home weakens the Administration in its fight for democracy three thousand miles away."

Of course, it was embarrassing. We meant it to be. We believed the truth must be told at all costs.

But others believed something must be done to stop the women. Hurried conferences were held behind closed doors. The military was summoned to discuss declaring a military zone around the White House. Closing the Woman's Party Headquarters was discussed but no reason could be found to justify the action.

Finally a decision was reached. The Chief of Police, Major Pullman, was sent to request us to stop picketing and to tell us that if we continued to picket, we would be arrested.

"We have picketed for six months without interference," said Miss Paul. *"Has the law been changed?"*

"No," was the reply, "but you must stop it."

"But, Major Pullman, we have consulted our lawyers and know we have a legal right to picket."

"I warn you, you will be arrested if you attempt to picket again."

The following day Lucy Burns and Katharine Morey of Boston carried to the White House gates the banner with the President's own words:

> WE SHALL FIGHT FOR THE THINGS WE HAVE ALWAYS HELD NEAREST OUR HEARTS, FOR DEMOCRACY, FOR THE RIGHT OF THOSE WHO SUBMIT TO AUTHORITY HAVE A VOICE IN THEIR OWN GOVERNMENT.

Police arrest suffrage pickets outside the White House, August 17, 1917. (Smithsonian Institution)

News had spread through the city that the pickets were to be arrested. A moderately large crowd had gathered to see the fun. Some members of the crowd made sport of the women. Others hurled cheap and childish epithets at them. Small boys were allowed to capture souvenirs, shreds of the banners torn from non-resistant women, as trophies.

Thinking they had been mistaken in believing the pickets were to be arrested, and having grown weary of their sport, the crowd moved on its way. Two solitary figures remained, standing on the sidewalk, looking quite abandoned and alone, when suddenly without any warrant in law, they were arrested on a completely deserted avenue.

Miss Burns and Miss Morey upon arriving at the police station insisted, to the great surprise of all the officials, upon knowing the charge against them. Major Pullman and his entire staff were utterly at a loss to know what to answer. The Administration had looked ahead only as far as threatening arrest. They doubtless thought this was all they would have to do. People could not be arrested for picketing. Picketing is a guaranteed right under the Clayton Act of Congress. Disorderly conduct? Inciting to riot? The women had merely stood as silent sentinels holding banners with the President's own eloquent words.

Hours passed. Finally the two prisoners were told that they had "obstructed the traffic" on Pennsylvania Avenue, were dismissed on their own recognizance, and were never brought to trial.

The following day, June 23, more arrests were made; two women at the White House, two at the Capitol. All carried banners with the same words of the President. There was no hesitation this time. They were promptly arrested for "obstructing the traffic." They, too, were dismissed and their cases never tried. It seemed clear that the Administration hoped to suppress picketing merely by arrests. When, however, women continued to picket in the face of arrest, the Administration quickened its advance into the venture of suppression. It decided to bring the offenders to trial.

On June 26, six American women were tried, judged guilty on the technical charge of "obstructing the traffic," warned by the court of their "unpatriotic, almost treasonable behavior," and sentenced to pay a fine of twenty-five dollars or serve three days in the District Jail.

"Not a dollar of your fine shall we pay," was the answer of the women. "To pay a fine would be an admission of guilt. We are innocent."

The six women who were privileged to serve the first terms of imprisonment for suffrage in this country, were Katharine Morey of Massachusetts, Annie Arneil and Mabel Vernon of Delaware, Lavinia Dock of Pennsylvania, Maud Jamison of Virginia, and Virginia Arnold of North Carolina.

On Independence Day, July 4, 1917, in front of the White House eleven women stood with banners bearing the words, GOVERNMENTS DERIVE THEIR JUST POWERS FROM THE CONSENT OF THE GOVERNED. They, too, were arrested, tried and sent to jail for "obstructing the traffic."

CHAPTER SEVEN

Occoquan Workhouse

ON JULY 14, the French holiday of Bastille Day, inspiring scenes and tragic sacrifices for liberty came to our minds. Sixteen women marched in single file from Headquarters to the White House gates. They carried a banner with the French motto: LIBERTY, EQUALITY, FRATERNITY. On that hot afternoon a thin line of curious spectators gathered in the park opposite suffrage Headquarters. The police closed in on the women and followed them to the gates.

Their proud banner was scarcely at the gates when the leader was placed under arrest. Her place was taken by another. She was taken. Another, and still another stepped into the breach and was arrested.

Meanwhile, the crowd grew, attracted by the presence of the police and the patrol wagon. There were sounds of applause, cries of "shame" for the police, and an occasional hoot from a small boy. But for the most part, an intense silence fell on the spectators, as they saw not only younger women but white-haired grandmothers hoisted into the crowded police vehicle, their heads erect and their frail hands holding tightly to the banner until wrested from them by superior force.

The following Monday the suffrage prisoners appeared in court to answer the charges against them. The women spoke briefly in their own defense.

Anne Martin began:

> This is what we are doing with our banners before the White House. We are asking the President of the United States to use

his great power to secure the passage of the national suffrage amendment. As long as the Government and the representatives of the Government prefer to send women to jail on petty and technical charges, we will go to jail. Our work for the passage of the amendment must go on. It will go on.

Mrs. John Rogers, Jr., descendant of Roger Sherman, one of the signers of the Declaration of Independence, continued:

We are not guilty of any offense. We know full well that we stand here because the President of the United States refuses to give liberty to American women.... The President puts his power behind all measures in which he takes a genuine interest. If he will say one frank word advocating this measure it will pass as a piece of war emergency legislation.

Florence Bayard Hilles spoke in her own defense:

What a spectacle it must be to the thinking people of this country to see us urged to go to war for democracy in a foreign land, and to see women thrown into prison who plead for that same cause at home. I stand here to affirm my innocence of the charge against me.... I shall continue to plead for the political liberty of American women—and especially do I plead to the President, since he is the one person who can end the struggles of American women to take their proper places in a true democracy.

There was continuous objection from the prosecutor, eager advice from the judge, and rounds of applause from the intent audience whenever a defiant note was struck by the prisoners. In spite of the sharp rapping of the gavel, confusion reigned.

Mrs. Gilson Gardner of Washington, D. C., a member of the Executive Committee of the National Woman's party, spoke:

It is impossible for me to believe that we were arrested because we were obstructing traffic or blocking the public highway. We have been carrying on activities of a distinctly political nature, and these political activities have seemingly disturbed certain powerful influences. Arrests followed. I submit that these arrests are purely political and that the charge of an unlawful assemblage and of obstructing traffic is a political subterfuge.

It was my task to sum up for the defense:

> We know and I believe the Court knows also that President Wilson and his Administration are responsible for our being here today. It is a fact that they gave the orders which caused our arrest and appearance before this bar.
>
> What is our real crime? What have these distinguished and liberty-loving women done to bring them before this court of justice? Why, your Honor, their crime is that they peacefully petitioned the President of the United States for liberty. What must be the shame of our nation before the world when it becomes known that here we throw women into jail who love liberty and attempt to peacefully petition the President for it? These women are nearly all descended from revolutionary ancestors or from some of the greatest libertarian statesmen this country has produced. What would these men say now if they could see that passion for liberty rewarded with foul and filthy imprisonment!
>
> We say to you, this outrageous policy of stupid and brutal punishment will not dampen the ardor of the women. Where sixteen of us face your judgment today there will be sixty tomorrow, so great will be the indignation of our colleagues in this fight.

The trial came to an end after a tense two days. The packed courtroom sat in a terrible silence awaiting the judge's verdict. After a delay, during which he reportedly consulted with the District Commissioners, the judge returned to pronounce, "Sixty days in the workhouse in default of a twenty-five dollar fine."

All in the courtroom were shocked. We would not of course pay the unjust fine imposed, for we were not guilty of any offense.

The judge attempted persuasion. It was clear that neither he nor those Administration leaders he had conferred with had imagined women would accept with equanimity so drastic a sentence as the workhouse.

"We protest against this unjust sentence and conviction," we said, "but we prefer the workhouse to the payment of a fine imposed for an offense of which we are not guilty." We filed into the "pen" to join other prisoners waiting to be carried off to prison.

We were all taken first to the District Jail and locked up, two to a cell. We learned then that the Occoquan workhouse, where we were to serve our sentences, was not situated in the District of Columbia but in neighboring Virginia.

Locked wagons with tiny windows took us along with drunks and disorderlies, prostitutes and thieves to the Pennsylvania Station. Here we embarked on the train for the unknown terrors of the workhouse, filing through the crowds at the station who were quick to realize that we were prisoners, because of our associates. Friends tried to bid us a last farewell and slip us a sweet or fruit, as we were rushed through the iron gates to the train.

It was almost totally dark when we arrived at a tiny station in what seemed to us a deserted wilderness. Even the bravest member of our party was struck with a little terror. More locked wagons awaited us. The prison van carried us over a rocky and hilly road. A cluster of lights twinkled beyond the last hill, and we knew that we were coming to our temporary summer residence. I can still see the long thin line of black poplars against the mouldering afterglow. I did not know then what tragic things they concealed.

The hard-faced matron, Mrs. Herndon, began the prison routine. Names were called, and each prisoner stepped to the desk to get her number, to give up all jewelry, money, handbags, letters, eye glasses, traveling bags containing toilet necessities, in fact everything except the clothes on her body.

From there we were herded into the long, bare dining room where we sat down to a bowl of dirty, sour soup. Now began the rule of silence. Prisoners are punished for speaking to one another at the table. They cannot even whisper, much less smile or laugh. We tasted our soup and crust of bread and tried so hard to eat it, for we were tired and hungry. But not one of us was able to get it down.

Another long march in silence brought us into a large dormitory with a double line of cots. There we stood, weary to the point of fainting, waiting the next ordeal. At that juncture, we lost all that remained of our contact with the outside world—our clothes. Each prisoner was obliged to strip naked without even the protection of a sheet, and to proceed to a shower bath. Naked, we returned from the bath to receive our allotment of coarse, hideous prison clothes. The outer garments consisted of a bulky mother-hubbard wrapper of bluish gray ticking and a heavy apron of the same dismal stuff. The thick unbleached muslin undergarments were of designs never to be forgotten. As were the thick stockings and forlorn shoes. What torture to put on shoes that are alike for each foot and made to fit any size.

Although it was long past the bedtime hour, we were told to dress and then were led into what we later learned was the "recreation" room. Lined up against its wall, we waited until Warden Whittaker came in.

The door finally opened and in came Warden Whittaker with a stranger beside him. He reviewed his latest criminal recruits, engaging the stranger in whispered conversation. There were short, uncertain laughs, nods of the head and more whispers.

"Well, ladies, I hope you are all comfortable. Now make yourselves at home here. I think you will find it healthy here. You'll weigh more when you go out than when you came in. You will be allowed to write one letter a month to your family. Of course we open and read all letters coming in and going out. Tomorrow you will be assigned your work. I hope you will sleep well. Good night."

We did not answer. We could only look at each other.

We tried very hard to sleep that night and to forget our hunger and weariness, but there was no sleep in this strange place.

Our thoughts turned to the outside world. Will the women care? Will enough women believe that through such humiliation all may win freedom? Will they believe that through our imprisonment their slavery will be lifted sooner? Will the Government be moved by public protest of our treatment? Will such protest come?

The next morning after our inedible breakfast, we were sent to work in the sewing room. Although conversing with the "regulars" was forbidden, we managed from time to time, to talk to our fellow prisoners.

"What yo'all down here for?" asked a young negress barely out of her teens.

"We all held purple, white and gold banners at the gates of the White House asking President Wilson to give us the vote. The President seemed to think it would be a good idea to send us to the workhouse for our actions."

"We knew something was goin' to happen," said another prisoner, "because Monday the clothes we had on were took off us and we were given these old patched ones.

"We heard they was bein' washed for you all suffragettes."

We were not convicted until Tuesday and yet our prison garments had been made ready on Monday!

That morning brought us a visitor from suffrage headquarters. The institution hoped that the visitor would persuade us to pay our fines and leave, and so she was admitted. We learned the cheering news that immediately after sentence had been pronounced by the Court, Dudley Field Malone, then Collector of the Port of New York, had gone direct to the White House to protest to the President. The President said that he was shocked at the sixty-day sentence, that he did not know it had been done, and made other evasions.

Following Mr. Malone, Mr. J. A. H. Hopkins, a member of the Democratic Campaign Committee of 1916, went to the White House and told the President of the conditions under which the women were being held. "How would you like to have your wife sleep in a dirty workhouse next to prostitutes?" Again the President was "shocked." No wonder! Mr. and Mrs. Hopkins recently had been the President's dinner guests, celebrating his return to power. They had supported him politically and financially, and now Mrs. Hopkins had been arrested at his gate and thrown into prison.

In reporting the interview, Mr. Hopkins said, "The President asked me for suggestions as to what might be done, and I replied that in view of the seriousness of the present situation the only solution lay in immediate passage of the Susan B. Anthony amendment."

Telegrams poured in from all over the country. The press printed headlines which could not but arouse the sympathy of thousands. Even people who did not approve of picketing the White House did not think our actions were bad enough to merit such drastic punishment.

And women protested. From coast to coast copies of telegrams sent to Administration leaders poured in at our Headquarters. Of course, not all women by any means had approved this method of agitation. But the Government's action had done more than we had been able to do. It had made women feel sex-conscious. Women were being unjustly treated. Regardless of their feelings about picketing, women stood up and objected to our treatment.

For the first time, I believe, our form of agitation began to seem a little more respectable than the Administration's handling of it. But the Administration did not yet realize this.

That night, when our untasted supper was over, we were ordered into the square, bare-walled recreation room, where we and the other prisoners sat, and sat, and sat, our chairs against the walls, waiting until bedtime. We tried to sing. The negroes joined in and soon outsang us with their plaintive melodies and hymns. Then back to our cells and another attempt to sleep.

We asked again and again to be given our toothbrushes, combs, handkerchiefs and soap. The third day of imprisonment without any of these essentials found us depressed and worried over our unsanitary condition. We pleaded also for toilet paper. It was senseless to deny these necessities.

The third afternoon we were summoned into the presence of Superintendent Whittaker and were told that we were to be pardoned by the President. It was clear that protest on the outside had been strong enough to precipitate action from the Government, although it had not been strong enough to force action on the suffrage amendment. Still, it was forcing some action and that was important.

It was sad to leave the other prisoners behind. Especially pathetic were the girls who helped us with our clothes. They whispered such eager appeals in our ears, telling us of their drastic sentences for trifling offenses and of the cruel punishment. It was hard to resist digressing into some form of prison reform, as that way lay our instincts, but our reason told us that we must first change the status of women.

As we were leaving the workhouse to return to Washington, we had an unexpected revelation of the official attitude toward our campaign. Addressing Lucy Burns, who had arrived to assist us, Superintendent Whittaker said angrily, "Now that you women are going away, I have something to say to *you*. The next lot of women who come here won't be treated with the same consideration that these women were."

The day following our release, Mrs. J. A. H. Hopkins carried a picket banner to the gates of the White House to test the validity of the pardon. Her banner read, WE DO NOT ASK PARDON FOR OUR-SELVES BUT JUSTICE FOR ALL AMERICAN WOMEN. A curious crowd stood watching the lone picket. The President passed through the gates and saluted. The police did not interfere.

Daily pickets resumed and no arrests followed for the moment.

It was now August, three months since the Senate Suffrage Committee authorized its chairman to report the measure to the Senate for action. The chairman, however, said he was too busy to make a report but that he would do so "in a reasonable time." So much for the situation in the Senate!

Mr. Edwin Y. Webb, chairman of the House Judiciary Committee, clearly stated that no action would be taken on woman suffrage in his committee under rules of the Democratic caucus unless the President requested it be treated as an emergency war measure. Here was frank admission that the President was responsible for any action on the amendment.

Now that we were again allowed to picket the White House, the Republicans seized the opportunity to embarrass their opponents by precipitating a bitter debate over the issue in the Senate.

It seemed that our picketing had stimulated some action in Congress, but what was needed now was still more provocative action from us.

CHAPTER EIGHT

August Riots

IMPRISONING WOMEN had met with considerable public disapproval and political embarrassment to the Administration. The presidential pardon did not end its embarrassment, however, as the pickets returned to their posts in steadily increasing numbers. Their presence at the gates was as unwanted now as it had been before the arrests and imprisonments, but the Administration had found no way to rid themselves of the pickets. As another month of picketing drew to an end, the Administration ventured to try other ways to stop it. Their methods became physically more brutal, politically more stupid, and lawless in the extreme.

In the meantime, the President had drafted millions of young American men to die on foreign soil for foreign democracy. He had issued a special appeal to women to give their work, their treasure and their sons to this enterprise. At the same time he stood obstinately in the way of our main objective, the passing of the Amendment, and it was our daily task vividly to remind him of that objective. It was our responsibility to compel decisive action from him.

Using the return of Envoy Elihu Root from his mission to Russia as another dramatic opportunity to speak to the President, we took to the picket line these mottoes:

TO ENVOY ROOT. YOU SAY THAT AMERICA MUST THROW ITS MANHOOD TO THE SUPPORT OF LIBERTY. WHOSE LIBERTY? THIS NATION IS NOT FREE. TWENTY MILLION WOMEN ARE DENIED BY THE PRESIDENT OF THE UNITED

STATES THE RIGHT TO REPRESENTATION IN THEIR OWN
GOVERNMENT.

TELL THE PRESIDENT THAT HE CANNOT FIGHT AGAINST
LIBERTY AT HOME WHILE HE TELLS US TO FIGHT FOR
LIBERTY ABROAD.

TELL HIM TO MAKE AMERICA SAFE FOR DEMOCRACY
BEFORE HE ASKS THE MOTHERS OF AMERICA TO THROW
THEIR SONS TO THE SUPPORT OF DEMOCRACY IN EUROPE.
ASK HIM HOW HE CAN REFUSE LIBERTY TO AMERICAN
CITIZENS WHEN HE IS FORCING MILLIONS OF AMERICAN
BOYS OUT OF THEIR COUNTRY TO DIE FOR LIBERTY.

We did not regard Mr. Wilson as our President. Since we had no
vote we felt that he had neither political nor moral claim to our allegiance. War had been made without our consent. Our fight was
becoming increasingly difficult—almost desperate. Here we were, a
band of women fighting with banners in the midst of a world armed
to the teeth. And so it was not very difficult to understand how the
women grew more resentful of a president's hypocrisy—so eager to
sacrifice life to the vague hope of liberty abroad, while refusing to
assist in the peaceful legislative steps which would lead to self-government in our own country. The President's constant oratory on freedom and democracy moved us to scorn. We decided on a protest so
militant as to shock not only the President but the public. We
inscribed on our banner what countless American women had long
thought in their hearts.

And so, on August 14, we submitted to the world, through the
picket line, this question:

KAISER WILSON. HAVE YOU FORGOTTEN HOW YOU SYMPA-
THIZED WITH THE POOR GERMANS BECAUSE THEY WERE
NOT SELF-GOVERNED? 20,000,000 AMERICAN WOMEN
ARE NOT SELF-GOVERNED. TAKE THE BEAM OUT OF YOUR
OWN EYE.

We did not expect public sympathy at this point. We knew that not
even the members of Congress who had occasionally called the Presi-

dent "autocrat," "kaiser," "king," and "czar" would approve of our action.

Nor was it expected that eager young boys, all agog to fight Germans, would be averse to attacking women. They were out to fight and such was the public hysteria that it did not exactly matter whom they fought.

And so those excited boys of the Army and Navy attacked the women and destroyed their banner. Another banner was brought up to take its place. This one met the same fate. A large crowd assembled in front of the White House, either to watch or to assist in the attacks. At the very moment when one banner was being snatched away and destroyed, President and Mrs. Wilson passed through the gate. We know that the President saw American women being attacked, while the police refused them protection.

Not a move was made by the police to control the growing crowd, and the violence escalated. As the throng moved between the White House and our Headquarters at Cameron House across the street, so many banners were destroyed that finally Lucy Burns, Virginia Arnold and Elizabeth Stuyvesant took those remaining to the second and third floor balconies of our building and hung them out. At this point there was not a picket left on the street. The crowd was clearly obstructing the traffic, but no attempt was made to move them back or to protect the women, some of whom were attacked by sailors on their own doorsteps.

Two police officers watched without interfering while three sailors leaned a ladder against the side of our building, climbed up to the second floor balcony, mounted the iron railing and tore down all banners and the American flag. One sailor administered a severe blow with his clenched fist to the face of a young woman.

"Why did you do that?" she demanded.

The man halted for a brief instant in obvious amazement and said, "I don't know." And with a violent wrench he tore the banner from her hands and ran down the ladder.

Lucy Burns was nearly dragged over the railing of the balcony by two other sailors. The mob watched with fascination while she swayed to and fro in her struggle. And still no attempt was made by the police to quell the riot!

The climax came in the late afternoon when a bullet was fired through one of the heavy glass windows of the second floor, embedding itself in the ceiling. Finally police reserves were summoned and in less than five minutes the crowd was pushed back and the street cleared. Thinking now that they could rely on the protection of the police, the women started for the White House with their banners. But the police just looked on while all the banners were destroyed a few paces from Headquarters. More banners went out—purple, white and gold ones. They, too, were destroyed before they reached the White House. Twenty-two lettered banners and fourteen tricolored banners were destroyed that day. This entire spectacle was enacted within a stone's throw of the White House.

On August 15 the pickets again attempted to take their posts on the line.

On this day one lettered banner and fifty purple, white and gold flags were destroyed by a mob led by sailors in uniform. Alice Paul was knocked down three times by a sailor and dragged the width of the White House sidewalk in his frenzied attempt to tear off her suffrage sash. Katharine Morey of Boston was shoved to the pavement by a sailor who took her flag. Elizabeth Stuyvesant was struck and her blouse torn from her body. Maud Jamison of Virginia was knocked down and dragged along the sidewalk. Beulah Amidon of North Dakota was also knocked down.

On August 16, fifty policemen led the mob in attacking the women. Hands were bruised and arms twisted by police officers and plainclothes men. Two civilians who tried to rescue the women from the attacks of the police were arrested. The police fell upon these young women with more brutality even than the mobs. Twenty-five lettered banners and 123 party flags were destroyed by mobs and police on this afternoon.

Finding that riots and mob attacks had not terrorized the women sufficiently to stop the pickets, the Administration decided again to arrest them in the hope of ending the agitation. Having lost public sympathy through workhouse sentences, having won it back by pardoning the women, the Administration felt it could afford to risk losing it again.

And so, on the morning of August 17, after three days of riotous attacks when it was clear that the pickets would persist, the Chief of Police called at Headquarters to warn Miss Paul that "orders have been changed and henceforth women carrying banners will be arrested." Alice Paul responded, "The pickets will go on as usual."

Throughout the early part of that afternoon, the silent sentinels stood unmolested at the White House gate. They carried these mottoes:

ENGLAND AND RUSSIA ARE ENFRANCHISING WOMEN IN WAR-TIME.

HOW LONG MUST WOMEN WAIT FOR LIBERTY?

THE GOVERNMENT ORDERS OUR BANNERS DESTROYED BECAUSE THEY TELL THE TRUTH.

At four o'clock the threatened arrests took place. Six women were quickly found guilty of "obstructing traffic" in a brief trial. None of the facts of the hideous and cruel manhandling by the mobs and police officers was allowed to be brought out. Nothing the women could say mattered. The judge pronounced: "Thirty days in Occoquan workhouse in lieu of a ten-dollar fine."

"College Day" on the picket line in front of the White House, 1917. (Smithsonian Institution)

And so this handful of women began the cruel sentence of thirty days in the workhouse, while their cowardly assailants were not even reprimanded, nor were those who destroyed over a thousand dollars' worth of banners apprehended.

Shortly after the incident of the "kaiser banner," I was speaking in Louisville, Kentucky. The auditorium was packed and overflowing with men and women who had come to hear the story of the pickets. Up to this time we had very few members in Kentucky and I had anticipated in this Southern state, part of President Wilson's stronghold, that our Committee would meet with no enthusiasm and possibly with hostility.

I had related briefly the incidents leading up to the picketing and the Government's suppressions. I was rather cautiously approaching the subject of the "kaiser banner," wondering how this vast audience of Southerners would take it. Slowly I read the inscription on the famous banner. I hardly reached the last word when a terrific outburst of applause came to my amazed ears.

A few minutes later a telegram was brought to the platform announcing the arrests and sentencing of six more women. As I read it aloud, instant cries of "Shame! Shame! It's an outrage!" rang out. Scores of men and women were on their feet calling for the passage of a resolution denouncing the Administration's policy of persecution. The motion of condemnation went through unanimously with prolonged shouts and applause.

The meeting continued late into the night, and I shall never forget that audience. Improvised collection baskets were piled high with bills. Women volunteered for picket duty and certain imprisonment, and the following day a delegation left for Washington.

This experience was typical. Every one of us who went through the country telling the story had similar experiences. Indignation was swift and hot. Our mass meetings everywhere became meetings of protest during the entire campaign. And the resolutions of protest which always went immediately by wire from such meetings to the President, his cabinet and to his leaders in Congress, created increasing uneasiness in Democratic circles.

The riots attracted sufficient attention, so that Congress was finally provoked into a little activity. Two attempts were made to introduce bills into the Senate that would prohibit picketing. Neither was successful.

Voices were also raised in our behalf. Gilson Gardner, whose wife had been among those pardoned in the first workhouse sentences, urged Major Pullman, the Chief of Police, to resign for allowing mob violence and for arresting suffragists. A resolution was introduced into the House which called for an investigation of conditions in the Capital that permitted mobs to attack women. The press throughout the entire country protested against mob violence and the severe sentences given the women.

Between these opposing currents of protest and support, the Administration drifted helplessly. Unwilling to pass the amendment, it continued to send women to prison.

On the afternoon of September 4, President Wilson led his first contingent of drafted "soldiers of freedom" down Pennsylvania Avenue in gala parade on the first lap of their journey to the battlefields of France. On the same afternoon a slender line of women, also "soldiers of freedom," attempted to march in Washington.

As the first two women came to take up their posts in front of the reviewing stand opposite the White House, they were swept away by the police like common street criminals, their golden banners scarcely flung to the breeze.

MR. PRESIDENT, HOW LONG MUST WOMEN BE DENIED A
VOICE IN A GOVERNMENT WHICH IS CONSCRIPTING THEIR
SONS?

Pennsylvania Avenue had been roped off for the parade. There was hardly any one passing at the time; all traffic had been temporarily suspended, so there was none to obstruct. But the Administration's policy of arrests must go on. A few moments later two more women marched down the avenue, their gay banners waving joyously in the autumn sun, to fill the gap of the two comrades who had been arrested. They, too, were shoved into the police automobile and hurried to the police station.

A third pair of pickets was arrested. Still others advanced. The crowd watched eagerly as the line of indomitable women continued to march, two by two, into the face of certain arrest. But still they came. Thirteen women were arrested and were sent to Occoquan for sixty days.

The Administration had not yet abandoned hope of removing the pickets. They persisted in their policy of arrests and longer imprisonments.

CHAPTER NINE

Prison Episodes

URING ALL THIS TIME the suffrage prisoners were enduring
the miserable and petty tyranny of the prison workhouse at
Occoquan. They were kept absolutely incommunicado. They were
not allowed to see even their nearest relatives until they had been in
the institution two weeks.

Each prisoner was allowed to write one outgoing letter a month,
which, after being read by the warden, could be sent or withheld at his
whim. All incoming mail and telegrams were also censored and practically all of them were denied to the prisoners.

As far as possible the women intended to abide by the routine of the
institution, disagreeable and unreasonable as it was. They performed
the tasks assigned to them. They ate the prison food without protest.
They wore the coarse prison clothes. But at the end of the first week of
detention they became so weak from the shockingly bad food that
they began to wonder if they could endure a diet of sour bread, half-
cooked vegetables, and rancid soup with worms in it.

The true condition of the prison began to travel to the outside
world through the devious routes of prison messengers. Senator J.
Hamilton Lewis of Illinois, Democratic whip in the Senate, thus
heard alarming reports of one of his constituents, Lucy Ewing,
daughter of a judge and niece of Adlai Stevenson (vice president in
Cleveland's Administration). He made a hurried trip to the workhouse to see her. The fastidious Senator was shocked at the appearance of the prisoners, shocked at the tale they told, shocked that
"ladies" should be subjected to such indignities.

Very soon afterwards the District Commissioners announced that an investigation of conditions in the workhouse would be held. As evidence an affidavit made by Mrs. Bovee, a prison matron who had been kind to the suffrage prisoners, was submitted to the Commissioners. It read in part:

> I am well acquainted with the conditions at Occoquan. I have had charge of all the suffragist prisoners who have been there. I know that their mail has been withheld from them.
>
> The blankets now being used in the prison have been in use since December without being washed or cleaned. Blankets are washed once a year. Officers are warned not to touch any of the bedding. The one officer who handles it is compelled by the regulations to wear rubber gloves while she does so....
>
> The beans, hominy, rice, cornmeal, and cereal have all had worms in them. Sometimes the worms float on top of the soup. Often they are found in the cornbread. The first suffragists sent the worms to Whittaker on a spoon.
>
> Prisoners are punished by being put on bread or water, or by being beaten. I know of one girl who has been kept seventeen days on only water this month in the "booby house." The same was kept nineteen days on water last year because she beat Superintendent Whittaker when he tried to beat her.
>
> Superintendent Whittaker or his son are the only ones who beat the girls. Officers are not allowed to lay a hand on them in punishment. I know of one girl beaten until the blood had to be scrubbed from her clothing and from the floor of the "booby house." I have never actually seen a girl beaten, but I have seen her afterward and the suffragists and I have heard the cries and blows.
>
> (Signed) Mrs. Virginia Bovee

While the Administration was planning an investigation of the conditions in the workhouse, which made it difficult for women to sustain health through a thirty-day sentence, more women were being arrested, tried and given sixty-day sentences, under the same conditions. The Administration did not understand the simple fact that women would not stop going to prison until something had been done which promised passage of the amendment through Congress.

Meanwhile, women in the workhouse suffered intimidation and hardship.

Mrs. Frederick Kendall of Buffalo, New York, was put in a "punishment cell" on bread and water, under a charge of "impudence." Her impudence consisted of protesting to the matron that scrubbing floors on her hands and knees was too severe work as she had been unable for days to eat the prison food.

She was refused the clean clothing she should have had the day she was put in solitary confinement and was thus forced to wear the same clothing eleven days. She was refused a nightdress or clean linen for the cot. Her only toilet accommodations was an open pail. For four days she was allowed no water for toilet purposes. Her diet consisted of three thin slices of bread and three cups of water, carried to her in a paper cup which frequently leaked out half the meager supply before it got to her cell.

Sewing room at Occoquan workhouse. (National Woman's Party)

Friends of Mrs. Kendall created a considerable disturbance when they learned of this cruel treatment, with the result that she was finally given clean clothing and taken from her confinement.

Lucy Burns was also placed on a bread and water diet for attempting to speak to Mrs. Kendall through her cell door to inquire after her health while in solitary.

It was such shocking facts as these that the Commissioners and their investigating board were vainly trying to keep from the country for the sake of the reputation of the Administration. But these revelations moved Jeannette Rankin of Montana, the only woman member of Congress, to introduce a resolution calling for a Congressional investigation of the workhouse.

But still the arrests continued and half a hundred women were sentenced in one month.

Through it all the women were ingenious at lifting the dull monotony of imprisonment. Locked in separate cells, the suffragists could still communicate by song. The prisoners would build a song, each calling out from cell to cell, and contributing a line. The following is part of a song written to the tune of "Charlie Is My Darling."

Shout the Revolution of Women

Shout the revolution
   Of women, of women,
Shout the revolution
   For liberty.
Rise, glorious women of the earth,
   The voiceless and the free
United strength assures the birth
   Of true democracy.

(Refrain)
Invincible our army,
   Forward, forward,
Triumphant daughters pressing
   To victory.

Sometimes it was the beautiful voice of Vida Milholland which rang through the corridors of the dreary prison, with a stirring Irish ballad, a French love song, or the "Woman's Marseillaise."

> *March on, march on.*
> *Face to the dawn,*
> *The dawn of liberty.*

The gaiety was interspersed with sadness when the suffragists learned of new cruelties heaped upon the helpless "regulars," those who were without influence or friends. They learned of that barbarous punishment known as "the greasy pole." This method of punishment consisted of strapping girls with their hands tied behind them to a greasy pole from which they were partly suspended. Unable to keep themselves in an upright position, because of the grease on the pole, they slipped almost to the floor, with their arms all but severed from the arm sockets, suffering intense pain for long periods of time. This cruel punishment was meted out to prisoners for slight infractions of the prison rules.

The suffrage prisoners learned also of the race hatred which the authorities encouraged. It was not infrequent that the jail officers summoned black girls to attack white women, if the latter disobeyed. This happened in one instance to the suffrage prisoners who were protesting against the warden's forcibly taking a suffragist from the workhouse without telling her or her comrades whither she was being taken. Black girls were called and commanded to attack the suffragists physically. The reluctant prisoners were goaded to deliver blows upon the women by the warden's threats of punishment.

Prison life was difficult but was endured for the cause. Katharine Fisher's speech given sometime later at a dinner in honor of released prisoners, describes the resolve of the women:

> Five of us who are with you tonight have recently come out from the workhouse into the world. A great change? Not so much of a change for women, disfranchised women. In prison or out, American women are not free. Our lot of physical freedom simply gives us and the public a new and vivid sense of what our lack of political freedom really means.

Disfranchisement is the prison of women's power and spirit. Women have long been classed with criminals so far as their voting rights are concerned. And how quick the Government is to live up to its classification the minute women determinedly insist upon these rights. Prison life epitomizes all life under undemocratic rule. At Occoquan, as at the Capitol and the White House, we faced hypocrisy, trickery and treachery on the part of those in power. And the constant appeal to us to cooperate with the workhouse authorities sounded wonderfully like the exhortation addressed to all women to support the Government.

"Is that the law of the District of Columbia?" I asked Superintendent Whittaker concerning a statement he had made to me. "It is the law," he answered, "because it is the rule I make." The answer of Whittaker is the answer Wilson makes to women every time the Government, of which he is the head, enacts a law and at the same time continues to refuse to pass the Susan B. Anthony amendment.

We seem today to stand before you free, but I have no sense of freedom because I have left comrades at Occoquan and because other comrades may at any moment join them there....

While comrades are there what is our freedom? It is as empty as the so-called political freedom of women who have won suffrage by a state referendum. Like them we are free only within limits....

We must not let our voice be drowned by war trumpets or cannon. If we do, we shall find ourselves, when the war is over, with a peace that will only prolong our struggle, a democracy that will belie its name by leaving out half the people.

The Administration continued to send women to the workhouse and the District Jail for thirty- and sixty-day sentences.

CHAPTER TEN

The Administration Yields

IN SEPTEMBER 1917 Dudley Field Malone, intimate friend and long-time political supporter of President Wilson, resigned his position as Collector of the Port of New York in protest of the Administration's handling of the suffrage issue.

In 1916 Mr. Malone had helped convince the women voters of the West to vote for President Wilson by promising them he would do everything in his power to get the Administration to pass the suffrage amendment. What happened instead was the arrest of peaceful women pickets on false charges and their illegal imprisonment.

In an interview, Mr. Malone stated:

> I cannot remain in office and see women thrown into jail because they demand their political freedom. The President may have been innocent of responsibility for the first arrests, but he was personally and politically responsible for all the arrests that occurred after his pardon of the first group. Under this development it seemed to me that self-respect demanded action, so I sent my resignation to the President, publicly stated my attitude and regretfully left his Administration.

Mr. Malone was shocked that the policy of arrests continued. Mr. Wilson and his Administration were shocked that anyone should care enough about the liberty of women to resign a lucrative post in the

Government. The nation was shocked into the realization that this was not a street brawl between women and policemen, but a controversy between suffragists and a powerful Administration. Mr. Malone did what we could only have done with the greatest difficulty and after more prolonged sacrifices. He laid the responsibility squarely and dramatically where it belonged. His fine, solitary and generous act accelerated the breakdown of the Administration's resistance. His sacrifice lightened ours.

In his letter of resignation, Mr. Malone wrote:

> It seems a long seven years, Mr. President, since I first campaigned with you when you were running for Governor of New Jersey. In every circumstance throughout those years I have served you with the most respectful affection and unshadowed devotion. It is no small sacrifice now for me, as a member of your Administration, to sever our political relationship. But I think it is high time that men in this generation, at some cost to themselves, stood up to battle for the national enfranchisement of women.

Women ought to be willing to make sacrifices for their own liberation, but for a man to have the courage and imagination to make such a sacrifice for the liberation of women is unparalleled. Mr. Malone called to the attention of the nation the true cause of the obstruction and suppression. He reproached the President and his colleagues in the most honorable way by refusing to associate himself with an Administration which backed such policies.

And Mr. Malone's protest was welcomed not only by the militant group of suffragists. More conservative suffrage leaders were equally outspoken in their gratitude, including Mrs. Carrie Chapman Catt, president of the National American Woman Suffrage Association, who heartily disapproved of picketing.

Immediately after Mr. Malone's sensational resignation, the Administration sought another way to remove the persistent pickets without passing the amendment.

Since the press had exposed the harsh prison regime we were undergoing, we were for the moment the object of sympathy, while the Administration was the butt of considerable hostility. Sensing their predicament and fearing any loss of prestige, they risked allowing a slight advance.

On September 14 Senator Andrieus A. Jones, Chairman of the Suffrage Committee, made a visit to the workhouse. Scarcely had the women recovered from the surprise of his visit when the Senator, on the following day, finally filed his report recommending passage by the Senate of the suffrage amendment. It had taken him exactly six months.

Next, the House of Representatives voted 181 to 107 in favor of creating a Committee on Woman Suffrage, all the time denying that the pickets had had anything to do with their action.

The creation of the Suffrage Committee in the House, pending since 1913, was finally granted in September 1917. To be sure this was accomplished only after an inordinate amount of time, money and effort had been spent on a sustained and relentless campaign of pressure. But the Administration had yielded.

As a means to remove the pickets, however, this was not enough. "We ask no more bureaucracy, no more committees and reports. We demand the passage of the amendment," said the pickets as they lengthened their line.

CHAPTER ELEVEN

Political Prisoners

FINDING THAT giving us a Suffrage Committee in the House and a report in the Senate had not silenced our banners, the Administration cast about for another plan by which to stop the picketing. This time they turned desperately to longer terms of imprisonment.

Our answer to this policy was more women on the picket line on the outside and a protest on the inside of prison.

We decided, in the face of extended imprisonment, to demand of the District Commissioners to be treated as political prisoners. We felt that, as a matter of principle, this was the dignified and self-respecting thing to do, since we had offended politically, not criminally. We believed further that a determined, organized effort to make clear to a wider public the political nature of the offense would intensify the Administration's embarrassment and so accelerate their final surrender.

It fell to Lucy Burns, vice chairman of the Woman's Party, to be the leader of the new protest inside the prison. With her red hair like a flaming torch and her body strong and vital, Miss Burns was the very symbol of woman in revolt. Without doubt she possessed the "voice" of the modern suffrage movement—she could move the most resistant person with her emotional quality and intellectual capacity. She was ideal for the stormy and courageous attack.

Miss Burns and Alice Paul first met in 1910 in a London police station, where they were among the hundred women arrested for attempting to present petitions for suffrage to Parliament, while they

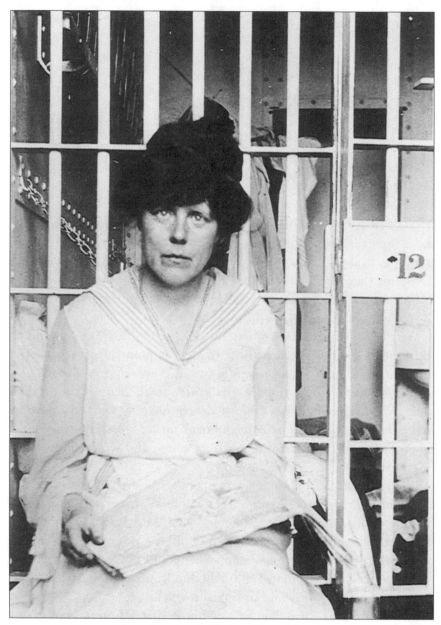

Lucy Burns in jail. (National Woman's Party)

were both students abroad. This was the first time either of them had participated in a demonstration, but from then on they worked together in England and Scotland organizing, speaking, heckling members of the Government, campaigning at elections; and going to prison together, where they joined the Englishwomen on hunger strike and where Miss Paul was forcibly fed.

In 1913 the two women undertook the leadership of the national suffrage work on the United States Congress. Throughout the entire campaign Miss Burns and Miss Paul counseled with one another on every point of any importance. This combination of the cool strategist and passionate rebel—each sharing some of the attributes of the other—has made for complete and unsurpassed leadership.

Lucy Burns had no sooner begun to organize her comrades for protest than the officials sensed a plot and removed her at once to solitary confinement. But they were too late. Taking the leader only hastened the rebellion. The initial demand to be treated as political prisoners was written on a forlorn piece of paper and was passed from prisoner to prisoner through holes in the wall surrounding leaden pipes, until a finished document had been perfected and signed by all the prisoners.

This historic document—historic because it represents the first organized group action ever made in America to establish the status of political prisoners—said:

> As political prisoners, we, the undersigned, refuse to work while in prison. We have taken this stand as a matter of principle after careful consideration, and from it we shall not recede.
>
> This action is a necessary protest against an unjust sentence. In reminding President Wilson of his pre-election promises toward woman suffrage we were exercising the right of peaceful petition, guaranteed by the Constitution of the United States, which declares peaceful picketing is legal in the District of Columbia. That we are unjustly sentenced has been well recognized—when President Wilson pardoned the first group of suffragists who had been given sixty days in the workhouse, and again when Judge Mullowny suspended sentence for the last

group of picketers. We wish to point out the inconsistency and injustice of our sentences—some of us have been given sixty days, a later group thirty days, and another group given a suspended sentence for exactly the same action.

Conscious, therefore, of having acted in accordance with the highest standards of citizenship, we ask the Commissioners of the District to grant us the rights due political prisoners. We ask that we no longer be segregated and confined under locks and bars in small groups, but permitted to see each other, and that Miss Lucy Burns, who is in full sympathy with this letter, be released from solitary confinement in another building and given back to us.

We ask exemption from prison work, that our legal right to consult counsel be recognized, to have food sent to us from outside, to supply ourselves with writing material for as much correspondence as we may need, to receive books, letters, newspapers, our relatives and friends.

Our united demand for political treatment has been delayed, because on entering the workhouse we found conditions so very bad that before we could ask that the suffragists be treated as political prisoners, it was necessary to make a stand for the ordinary rights of human beings for all the inmates. Although this has not been accomplished, we now wish to bring the important question of the status of political prisoners to the attention of the commissioners, who, we are informed, have full authority to make what regulations they please for the District prison and workhouse.

The Commissioners are requested to send us a written reply so that we may be sure this protest has reached them.

The Commissioners' only answer to this was a hasty transfer of the signers and the leader, Lucy Burns, to the District Jail, where they were put in solitary confinement. The women were not only refused the privileges asked but were denied some of the usual privileges allowed to ordinary criminals.

Generous publicity was given to these reasonable demands, and a surprisingly widespread protest followed the official denial of them.

Scores of committees went to the District Commissioners. Telegrams backing up the women's demand again poured in upon all the Administration.

Maria Moravsky, a Russian author and poet who had herself been imprisoned in czarist Russia and who was touring America at the time of this controversy, expressed her surprise that our suffrage prisoners should be treated as common criminals. She wrote:

> I have been twice in the Russian prison; life in solitary cell was not sweet; but I can assure you it was better than that which American women suffragists must bear. We were permitted to read and write; we wore our own clothes; we were not forced to mix with the criminals; we did no work. (Only a few women exiled to Siberia for extremely serious political crimes were compelled to work.) And our guardians and even judges respected us; they felt we were victims, because we struggled for liberty.

The Commissioners, who had to bear the responsibility of an answer to these protests and to the demand of the prisoners, contended to all that political prisoners did not exist in this country.

In response, we cited definitions of political offenses. We declared that all authorities on political crime sustained our contention that we clearly came under the category of political prisoners. We called to their attention the established custom of special treatment of political prisoners in other countries.

There can be no doubt in the official mind that our claim was just. But the Administration would not grant this demand and continued to persuade public opinion that our offense was not of a political nature; that it was nothing more than unpleasant and unfortunate riotous conduct in the Capital. Our demand to be treated as political prisoners was never granted, but it was kept up until the last imprisonment.

Our suffrage prisoners, however, made an important contribution toward establishing this reform. They were the first in America to organize and sustain this demand over an extended period of time. In our country we maintain a most backward policy in dealing with political prisoners. We have neither regulation nor precedent for special treatment of them.

CHAPTER TWELVE

Alice Paul in Prison

THE SPECIAL SESSION of the Sixty-fifth Congress, known as the "War Congress," adjourned in October 1917, having passed every measure recommended as a war measure by the President.

In addition it found time to protect by law migratory birds, to appropriate forty-seven million dollars for deepening rivers and harbors, and to establish more federal judgeships. No honest person would say that lack of time and pressure of war legislation had prevented its consideration of the suffrage measure. Week after week Congress met only for three days, and then often merely for prayer and a few hours of purposeless talking.

We had asked for liberty and had got a suffrage committee appointed in the House and a favorable report in the Senate from the Committee on Woman Suffrage, nothing more.

On the very day and hour of the adjournment of the special session of the War Congress, Alice Paul led eleven women to the White House gates to protest against the Administration's allowing its lawmakers to go home without action on the suffrage amendment. The women were arrested, and two days later Alice Paul and her colleagues came to trial.

Judge Mullowny cleared his throat. "Will the prisoners stand up and be sworn?" They would not.

"Will they speak in their own behalf?"

Miss Paul rose from her seat and said calmly, "We do not wish to

111

Alice Paul leads pickets from the Woman's Party headquarters towards the White House, October 1917. (National Woman's Party)

make any plea before this court. We do not consider ourselves subject to this court, since as an unenfranchised class we have nothing to do with the making of the laws which have put us in this position."

Although the women were quickly found guilty, their sentence was suspended "for the time being."

Was it that they did not dare confine Miss Paul? Were they beginning actually to perceive the real strength of the movement and the protest that would be aroused if she were imprisoned? Again we thought perhaps this marked the end of the jailing of women.

Still there was no indication that the Administration was ready to act on the amendment. And so, the pickets, including Miss Paul and others on suspended sentences, as well as first time offenders, again marched to the White House gates. All were arrested and brought to trial.

"You ladies seem to feel that we discriminate in making arrests and in sentencing you," said the judge heavily. "The result is that you force me to take the most drastic means in my power to compel you to obey the law."

The first offenders were given sentences of six months, while the others were to serve an additional month.

Miss Paul's parting remark to the reporters who intercepted her on her way from the courtroom to begin her seven months' sentence was: "We are being imprisoned, not because we obstructed traffic, but because we pointed out to the President the fact that he was obstructing the cause of democracy at home, while Americans were fighting for it abroad."

Alice Paul told me her story of what happened in the District Jail:

> It was late afternoon when we arrived at the jail. There we found the suffragists who had preceded us, locked in cells with no fresh air. Every window was closed tight. The air in which we would be obliged to sleep was foul. There were about eighty prisoners crowded together, tier upon tier. I went to a window and tried to open it. Instantly a group of men, prison guards, appeared; picked me up bodily, threw me into a cell and locked the door. Rose Winslow and the others were treated in the same way.
>
> Determined to preserve our health and that of the other prisoners, we began a concerted fight for fresh air. The windows were about twenty feet distant from the cells, and two sets of iron bars intervened between us and the windows, but we instituted an attack upon them as best we could. Our tin drinking cups, the electric light bulbs, every available article of the meager supply in each cell, including my treasured copy of Browning's poems which I had secretly taken in with me, was thrown through the windows. We finally succeeded in breaking one window. The fresh October air came in like an exhilarating gale.
>
> The next day we organized ourselves into a little group for the purpose of rebellion. We determined to make it impossible to keep us in jail. We determined, moreover, that as long as we were there we would keep up an unremitting fight for the rights of political prisoners....

There is absolutely no privacy allowed a prisoner in a cell. You are suddenly peered at by curious strangers, who look in at you all hours of the day and night, by officials, by attendants, by interested philanthropic visitors, and by prison reformers, until one's sense of privacy is so outraged that one rises in rebellion. We set out to secure privacy, but we did not succeed, for to allow privacy in prison is against all institutional thought and habit. Our only available weapon was our blanket, which was no sooner put in front of our bars than it was forcibly taken down by Warden Zinkhan.

Our meals consisted of a little almost raw salt pork, some sort of liquid—I am not sure whether it was coffee or soup—bread and occasionally molasses. How we cherished the bread and molasses, as almost every one was unable to eat the raw pork. Lucy Branham, who was more valiant than the rest of us, called out from her cell, one day, "Shut your eyes tight, close your mouth over the pork and swallow it without chewing it. Then you can do it." This heroic practice kept Miss Branham in fairly good health, but to the rest it seemed impossible, even with our eyes closed, to crunch our teeth into the raw pork.

However gaily you start out in prison to keep up a rebellious protest, it is nevertheless a terribly difficult thing to do in the face of the constant cold and hunger of undernourishment. Bread and water, and occasional molasses, is not a diet destined to sustain rebellion long. And soon weakness overtook us.

At the end of two weeks of solitary confinement, without any exercise, without going outside of our cells, some of the prisoners were released, having finished their terms, but seven of us were left. With our number thus diminished, the authorities felt able to cope with us. The doors were unlocked and we were permitted to take exercise. Rose Winslow fainted as soon as she got into the yard, and was carried back to her cell. I was too weak to move from my bed. Rose and I were taken on stretchers that night to the hospital.

For one brief night we occupied beds in the same ward in the hospital. Here we decided upon the hunger strike, as the ultimate form of protest left us—the strongest weapon left with which to continue within the prison our battle against the Administration.

From the moment we undertook the hunger strike, a policy of unremitting intimidation began. One authority after another, high and low, in and out of prison, came to attempt to force me to break the hunger strike.

"You will be taken to a very unpleasant place if you don't stop this," was a favorite threat of the prison officials, as they would hint vaguely of the psychopathic ward, and St. Elizabeth's, the Government insane asylum. They alternately bullied and hinted. Another threat was "You will be forcibly fed immediately if you don't stop"—this from Dr. Gannon, the jail physician.

After about three days of the hunger strike a man entered my room in the hospital and announced himself as Dr. White, the head of St. Elizabeth's. He said that he had been asked by District Commissioner Gardner to make an investigation.

"Please talk," said Dr. White. "Tell me about suffrage; why you have opposed the President; the whole history of your campaign, why you picket, what you hope to accomplish by it. Just talk freely."

"Indeed I'll talk," I said gaily, not having the faintest idea that this was an investigation of my sanity.

I drew myself together, sat upright in bed, propped myself up for a discourse of some length, and began to talk. The stenographer whom Dr. White brought with him took down in shorthand everything that was said.

I may say it was one of the best speeches I ever made. I recited the long history and struggle of the suffrage movement from its early beginning and narrated the political theory of our activities up to the present moment, outlining the status of the suffrage amendment in Congress at that time. In short, I told him everything. He listened attentively, interrupting only occasionally to say, "But, has not President Wilson treated you women very badly?" Whereupon, I, still unaware that I was being examined, launched forth into an explanation of Mr. Wilson's political situation and the difficulties he had confronting him. I continued to explain why we felt our relief lay with him; I cited his extraordinary power, his influence over his party, his undisputed leadership in the country, always painstakingly explaining that we opposed President Wilson merely because he happened to be President, not because he was President Wilson. Again came an interruption from Dr. White, "But isn't President Wilson directly responsible for the abuses and indignities which have been heaped upon you? You are suffering now as a result of his brutality, are you not?" Again I explained that it was impossible for us to know whether President Wilson was personally acquainted in any detail with the facts of our present condition, even though we knew that he had concurred in the early decision to arrest our women.

Presently Dr. White took out a small light and held it up to my eyes. Suddenly it dawned upon me that he was examining me personally; that his interest in the suffrage agitation and the jail conditions did not exist, and that he was merely interested in my reactions to the agitation and to jail. Even then I was reluctant to believe that I was the subject of mental investigation and I continued to talk.

But he continued in what I realized with a sudden shock, was an attempt to discover in me symptoms of the persecution mania. How simple he had apparently thought it would be, to prove that I had an obsession on the subject of President Wilson!

The day following he came again, this time bringing with him the District Commissioner, Mr. Gardner, to whom he asked me to repeat everything that had been said the day before. Then came another psychiatrist, Dr. Hickling, attached to the psychopathic ward in the District Jail, with more threats and suggestions, if the hunger strike continued. Finally they departed, and I was left to wonder what would happen next. Doubtless my sense of humor helped me, but I confess I was not without fear of this mysterious place which they continued to threaten.

It appeared clear that it was their intention either to discredit me, as the leader of the agitation, by casting doubt upon my san-

ity, or else to intimidate us into retreating from the hunger
strike.

Commissioner Gardner then made another visit. "All these
things you say about the prison conditions may be true," said Mr.
Gardner. "You give an account of a very serious situation in the
jail. The jail authorities give exactly the opposite. Now I promise
you we will start an investigation at once to see who is right, you
or they. If you will give up the hunger strike, we will start the
investigation at once."

"Will you consent to treat the suffragists as political prisoners,
in accordance with the demands laid before you?" I replied.

Commissioner Gardner refused, and I told him that the
hunger strike would not be abandoned. But they had by no
means exhausted every possible facility for breaking down our
resistance. I overheard the Commissioner say to Dr. Gannon on
leaving, "Go ahead, take her and feed her."

I was thereupon put upon a stretcher and carried into the psychopathic ward. There were two windows in the room. Dr. Gannon immediately ordered one window nailed from top to bottom. He then ordered the door leading into the hallway taken
down and an iron-barred cell door put in its place. He departed
with the command to a nurse to "observe her."

Following this direction, all through the day once every hour,
the nurse came to "observe" me. All through the night, once
every hour she came in, turned on an electric light sharp in my
face, and "observed" me. This ordeal was the most terrible torture, as it prevented my sleeping for more than a few minutes at
a time. And if I did finally get to sleep it was only to be shocked
immediately into wide-awakeness with the pitiless light.

It is scarcely possible to convey one's reaction to such an atmosphere. Here I was surrounded by people on their way to the insane
asylum. Some were waiting for their commitment papers. Others
had just gotten them. And all the while everything possible was
done to attempt to make me feel that I too was a "mental patient."

The nurses explained to me the procedure of sending a person
to the insane asylum. Two psychiatrists examine a patient in the

psychopathic ward, sign an order committing the patient to St. Elizabeth's Asylum, and there the patient is sent at the end of one week. No trial, no counsel, no protest from the outside world. This was the customary procedure.

I began to think that this was probably their plan for me. I could not see my family or friends; counsel was denied me; I saw no other prisoners and heard nothing of them; I could see no papers; I was entirely in the hands of doctors, prison officials and hospital staff.

I believe I have never in my life before feared anything or any human being. But I confess I was afraid of Dr. Gannon, the jail physician. I dreaded the hour of his visit.

At this time forcible feeding began in the District Jail. Alice Paul and Rose Winslow, the first two suffragists to undertake the hunger strike, went through the operation of forcible feeding three times a day until their release. The hunger strike spread immediately to other suffrage prisoners in the jail and to the workhouse.

While in the prison hospital, Miss Winslow wrote dramatic descriptions of the forcible feedings. Scribbled on tiny scraps of paper, Miss Winslow's notes were smuggled out to us and to her husband during her imprisonment.

Alice Paul is in the psychopathic ward. She dreaded forcible feeding frightfully, and I hate to think how she must be feeling. I had a nervous time of it, gasping a long time afterward, and my stomach rejecting during the process. I spent a bad, restless night, but otherwise I am all right. The poor soul who fed me got liberally besprinkled during the process. I heard myself making the most hideous sounds.... One feels so forsaken when one lies prone and people shove a pipe down one's stomach.

Yesterday was a bad day for me in feeding. I was vomiting continually during the process. The tube has developed an irritation somewhere that is painful.

Never was there a sentence like ours for such an offense as ours, even in England. No woman ever got it over there even for tearing down buildings. And during all that agitation we were busy saying that never would such things happen in the United States. The men told us they would not endure such frightfulness.

The same doctor feeds both Alice Paul and me. Don't let them tell you we take this well. Miss Paul vomits much. I do too. It's the nervous reaction, and I can't control it much. We think of the coming feeding all day. It is horrible. The doctor thinks I take it well. I hate the thought of Alice Paul and the others if I take it well.

All the officers here know we are making this hunger strike so that women fighting for liberty may be considered political prisoners; we have told them. God knows we don't want other women ever to have to do this over again.

CHAPTER THIRTEEN

Administration Terrorism

T HE ADMINISTRATION tried to stop the picketing by sentencing Alice Paul to the absurd and desperate sentence of seven months in jail for "obstructing traffic." They thought the agitation would certainly weaken with our leader safely behind the bars for so long a time. To their great surprise, however, in the face of that reckless and extreme sentence, the longest picket line of the entire campaign formed at the White House in the late afternoon of November 10, 1917. Forty-one women bearing gold-lettered banners and purple, white and gold flags picketed in protest against this wanton persecution of their leader, as well as against the delay in passing the amendment.

They were arrested, found guilty, but were summarily released without sentence.

The Administration did not relish the incarceration of an additional forty-one women from sixteen different states, partly because of limited jail accommodations, but also because they feared political repercussions. The women, however, were determined to force the Administration to take its choice. It could allow them to continue their peaceful agitation or it could stand the reaction which was bound to come from imprisoning them. And so the women returned to the White House gates to resume their picketing.

Again they were arrested, but the next day the women were told to come back later, that the judge was not yet ready to try the case. Using their welcome release to continue their protest, the women again marched with their banners to the White House in an attempt to picket. Again they were arrested. On the following morning they were given sentences ranging from six days to six months in prison. Lucy Burns received six months.

In pronouncing the lightest sentence upon Mrs. Mary Nolan, the judge said that he did so on account of her age of seventy-three years. He urged her, however, to pay her fine, hinting that jail might be too severe on her and might bring on death. At this suggestion, tiny, frail Mrs. Nolan pulled herself up on her toes and said with great dignity, "Your Honor, I have a nephew fighting for democracy in France. He is offering his life for his country. I should be ashamed if I did not join these brave women in their fight for democracy in America. I should be proud of the honor to die in prison for the liberty of American women."

In spite of the fact that the women were sentenced to serve their sentences in the District Jail, where they would join Miss Paul and her companions, all save one were immediately sent to Occoquan workhouse.

It had been agreed that the demand to be treated as political prisoners, inaugurated by previous pickets, should be continued, and that failing to secure such rights they would unanimously refuse to eat food or do prison labor. They would go on hunger strike as Alice Paul and the others were doing in the District Jail.

Mrs. Nolan tells of the prisoners' reception at the Occoquan workhouse:

> It was about half past seven at night when we got to Occoquan workhouse. Mrs. Lawrence Lewis, who spoke for all of us, said she must speak to Whittaker, the superintendent of the place....
>
> Suddenly the door literally burst open and Whittaker burst in like a tornado; some men followed him. We could see a crowd of them on the porch. They were not in uniform. Mrs. Lewis stood

up. Some of us had been sitting and lying on the floor, we were so tired. She had hardly begun to speak, saying we demanded to be treated as political prisoners, when Whittaker said, "You shut up. I have men here to handle you." Then he shouted, "Seize her!" I turned and saw men spring toward her, and then someone screamed, "They have taken Mrs. Lewis."

A man sprang at me and caught me by the shoulder. I remember saying, "I'll come with you; don't drag me; I have a lame foot." But I was jerked down the steps and away into the dark. I didn't have my feet on the ground. I guess that saved me.

The building to which they took us was lighted up as we came to it.... We were rushed into a large room that opened on a large hall with stone cells on each side. They were perfectly dark. Punishment cells is what they call them. Mine was filthy. It had no window save a slip at the top and no furniture but an iron bed covered with a thin straw pad, and an open toilet flushed from outside the cell....

I saw Dorothy Day brought in. She is a frail girl. The two men handling her were twisting her arms above her head. Then suddenly they lifted her up and banged her down over the arm of an iron bench—twice....

At the end of the corridor they pushed me through a door. Then I lost my balance and fell against the iron bed. Mrs. Cosu struck the wall. Then they threw in two mats and two dirty blankets. There was no light but from the corridor. The door was barred from top to bottom. The walls and floors were brick or stone cemented over. Mrs. Cosu put me on the couch and stretched out on the floor on one of the two pads they threw in. We had only lain there a few minutes, trying to get our breath, when Mrs. Lewis was literally thrown in. Her head struck the iron bed. We thought she was dead. She didn't move. We were crying over her as we lifted her to the pad on my bed, when Mr. Whittaker came to the door and told us not to dare to speak, or he would put the brace and bit in our mouths and the straitjacket on our bodies. We were so terrified we kept very still. Mrs. Lewis was not unconscious; she was only stunned. But Mrs. Cosu was desperately ill as the night wore on. She had a bad heart attack and was then vomiting. We called and called. We asked them to send our own doctor, because we thought she was dying.... The guards paid no attention. A cold wind blew in on us from the outside, and we three lay there shivering and only half conscious until morning.

Because of my age, I was then taken to the hospital cottage. I just lay down on a bed and fell into a kind of stupor. It was nearly noon and I had had no food offered me since the sandwiches our friends brought us in the courtroom at noon the day before. The doctor came and examined my heart. Then he examined my lame foot. It had a long blue bruise above the ankle, where they had knocked me as they took me across the night before.

The next day they brought me some toast and a plate of food, the first I had been offered in over thirty-six hours. I just looked at the food and motioned it away. It made me sick.... I was released on the sixth day.

The day following their commitment to Occoquan, our attorney Mr. Matthew O'Brien attempted to see the women to ascertain their condition, but he was denied admission.

The next day he again attempted to see his clients, as did the mother of Matilda Young, at nineteen years of age the youngest prisoner in Mr. Whittaker's care, and the mother of another prisoner. Admission was denied to all of them.

The terrible anxiety at Headquarters was not relieved the third day by a report brought from the workhouse by one of the marines stationed at Quantico Station, Virginia, who had been summoned to the workhouse on the night the women arrived. He brought news that unknown tortures were going on. Mr. O'Brien immediately forced his way into the prison by a court order, and brought back to Headquarters the astounding news of the campaign of terrorism which had started the moment the prisoners had arrived.

On the seventh day of their hunger strike, when Lucy Burns and Mrs. Lawrence Lewis were so weak that Mr. Whittaker feared their death, they were forcibly fed and taken immediately to the jail in Washington.

Lucy Burns wrote of her experience on tiny scraps of paper which were smuggled out of jail:

> Wednesday, 12 midnight. Yesterday afternoon at about four or five, Mrs. Lewis and I were asked to go to the operating room. Went there and Dr. Gannon told me then I must be fed. Was stretched on bed, two doctors, matron, four colored prisoners present, Whittaker in hall. I was held down by five people at legs, arms, and head. I refused to open mouth. Gannon pushed tube up left nostril. I turned and twisted my head all I could, but he managed to push it up. It hurts nose and throat very much and makes nose bleed freely. Tube drawn out covered with blood. Operation leaves one very sick. Food dumped directly into stomach feels like a ball of lead. Left nostril, throat and muscles of neck very sore all night. After this I was brought into the hospital in an ambulance. Mrs. Lewis and I placed in same room. Slept hardly at all. This morning Dr. Ladd appeared with his tube. Mrs. Lewis and I said we would not be forcibly fed. Said he would call in men guards and force us to submit. Went away and we were not fed at all this morning. We hear them outside now cracking eggs.

Mrs. Lewis later wrote:

> I was seized and laid on my back, where five people held me, a young colored woman leaping upon my knees, which seemed to break under the weight. Dr. Gannon then forced the tube through my lips and down my throat, I gasping and suffocating with the agony of it. I didn't know where to breathe from and everything turned black when the fluid began pouring in. I was moaning and making the most awful sounds quite against my will, for I did not wish to disturb my friends in the next room. Finally the tube was withdrawn. I lay motionless. After a while I was dressed and carried in a chair to a waiting automobile, laid on the back seat and driven into Washington to the jail hospital.

With Miss Burns and Mrs. Lewis, who were regarded as leaders in the hunger strike protest, removed to the District Jail, Mr. Whittaker and his staff at Occoquan began a systematic attempt to break down the morale of the hunger strikers. Each one was interrogated.

"Will you work?" "Will you put on prison clothes?" "Will you eat?" "Will you stop picketing?" "Will you go without paying your fine and promise never to picket again?" Each woman was firm in her refusal.

One of the few warming incidents during the gray days of our imprisonment was the unexpected sympathy and understanding of one of the Government doctors. "This is the most magnificent sacrifice I have ever seen made for a principle," he said. "I never believed that American women would care so much about freedom. I have seen women in Russia undergo extreme suffering for their ideals, but unless I had seen this with my own eyes I never would have believed it. You girls are on your ninth day of hunger strike and your condition is critical. It is a great pity that such women should be subjected to this treatment. I hope you will carry your point and force the hand of the Government soon."

Every conceivable lie was tried in an effort to force the women to abandon their various forms of resistance. They were told that no efforts were being made from the outside to reach them, and that their attorney had been called off the case. Each one was told that she was the only one hunger striking. Each one was told that all the others had put on prison clothes and were working. Although they were separated from one another they suspected the lies and remained strong in their resistance.

The judge had sentenced these women to the jail, but the District Commissioners had ordered them committed to the workhouse. It was evident that the Administration was anxious to keep this group away from Alice Paul and her companions, as they counted on handling the rebellion more easily in two groups than one.

Meanwhile the condition of the prisoners in the workhouse grew steadily worse. It was imperative that we force the Administration to remove them from the custody of Superintendent Whittaker immediately. We decided to take the only course left open to us—to obtain a writ of habeas corpus. The writ would compel the Government to bring the prisoners into court and show cause why they should not be returned to the District Jail.

There followed a week more melodramatic than the most stirring moving picture film. Although the writ had been applied for in the greatest secrecy, it was evident that the Administration was cognizant of every move in this procedure before it was executed. No sooner was our plan decided upon than friends of the Administration besought us to abandon the habeas corpus proceedings. "If you will only drop these proceedings, I can absolutely guarantee you that the prisoners will be removed from the workhouse to the jail in a week," was the appeal.

"In a week? They may be dead by that time," we answered. "We cannot wait."

There were three reasons why the authorities wished for a week's time. They were afraid to move the women in their weakened condition and they hoped to increase their facilities for forcible feeding at the workhouse by the end of the week. They also wished to conceal the treatment of the women, the exposure of which would be inevitable in any court proceedings. And lastly, the Administration was anxious to avoid opening up the whole question of the legality of the very sentence of the workhouse in Virginia.

Persons convicted in the District for acts committed in violation of District law were transported to Virginia—alien territory—to serve their terms. Eminent jurists held that the District had no right to convict a person under its laws and commit that person to confinement in another state. They contended that sentence imposed upon a person for unlawful acts in the District should be carried out in the District.

Hundreds of persons who had been convicted in the District of Columbia and who had served their sentences in Virginia had been without money or influence enough to contest this doubtful procedure in the courts, but we were prepared to do so. The Administration was alarmed.

We began at once to serve the writ upon Superintendent Whittaker. Ordinarily this would be an easy thing to do, but for us it developed into a very difficult task. A deputy marshal must serve a writ, but for miles around Washington, suddenly not one was to be found at his home or lodgings and none could be reached by telephone.

Meanwhile, Mr. Whittaker had fled from the premises of the work-house to the District, where he kept himself discreetly hidden for several days. When a deputy was finally found, six attempts were made to serve the writ. All failed. Finally by a ruse, Mr. Whittaker was caught at his home late at night. He was aroused to a state of violent temper and made futile threats of reprisal when he learned that he must produce the suffrage prisoners at the Court in Alexandria, Virginia, on the day of November 23.

CHAPTER FOURTEEN

The Administration Outwitted

O N NOVEMBER 23, 1917, the trial took place on our writ of habeas corpus. No one present can ever forget the scene enacted in the little Virginia courthouse that cold, dark morning. Present were Judge Edmund Waddill, a mild-mannered Southern gentleman, Superintendent Whittaker in his best Sunday clothes, Mrs. Herndon, the workhouse matron, and Warden Zinkhan of the District Jail, looking worried at the prospect of the prisoners being committed to him. Our counsels Dudley Field Malone and Matthew O'Brien were ready to try the case. The bevy of newspaper reporters struggled for places in the little courtroom, as did the many eager spectators.

All the people there experienced a shock when the slender file of women, haggard, red-eyed, sick, came to the bar. Some were able to walk to their seats; others were so weak that they had to be stretched out on the wooden benches with coats propped under their heads for pillows. Still others bore the marks of the attack on the "night of terror." Many of the prisoners lay back in their chairs hardly conscious of the proceedings which were intended to free them from Whittaker's control.

The purpose of the trial was to determine the legality of the act by the District Commissioners in sending prisoners to the Occoquan workhouse in Virginia when no formal transfer from one institution to another had been made and when the sentencing papers distinctly stated that all prisoners were to be committed to the Washington Jail.

It did not take Judge Waddill long to rule that the transfer was in fact carried out without legal process of any kind and that all the petitioners were to be removed from the workhouse and remanded to the custody of the Washington Jail.

The workhouse prisoners were thus taken to the District Jail to finish their sentences. There they joined Alice Paul and Rose Winslow and their comrades in continuing their hunger strike.

With thirty determined women on hunger strike, of whom eight were in a state of almost total collapse, the Administration capitulated. It could not afford to feed thirty women forcibly and risk the social and political consequences; nor could it let thirty women starve themselves to death, and likewise take the consequences. For by this time one thing was clear, and that was that the discipline and endurance of the women could not be broken. The doors of the jail were suddenly opened, and all suffrage prisoners were unconditionally released on November 27 and November 28.

With extraordinary swiftness the Administration's almost incredible policy of intimidation had collapsed. Miss Paul had been given a sentence of seven months, and at the end of five weeks the Administration was forced to acknowledge defeat.

On leaving prison Miss Paul said: "The commutation of sentences acknowledges them to be unjust and arbitrary. The attempt to suppress legitimate propaganda has failed. We hope that no more demonstrations will be necessary, that the amendment will move steadily on to passage and ratification without further suffering or sacrifice. But what we do depends entirely upon what the Administration does. We have one aim: the immediate passage of the federal amendment."

Running parallel to the protest going on inside the prison, a public protest of nationwide proportions had been made against continuing to imprison women. Deputations of influential women had waited upon all party leaders, cabinet officials, heads of the war boards, in fact every friend of the Administration, pointing out that we had broken no law, that we were unjustly held, and that the Administration would suffer politically for their handling of the suffrage agitation.

Congress reconvened on December 4. President Wilson delivered a message, restating our aims in the war. He also recommended a declaration of war against Austria; the control of certain water power sites; export trade combination; railway legislation; and the speeding up of all necessary appropriation legislation. But he did not mention the suffrage amendment. He had been forced to release the prisoners, but still he did nothing.

Immediately we called a conference in Washington of the Executive Committee and the National Advisory Council of the Woman's Party. A rumor that the President would soon act persisted, but we could not rely on rumor. We decided to accelerate him and his Administration by filing damage suits amounting to $800,000 against the District Commissioners, against Warden Zinkhan, against Superintendent Whittaker and Captain Reams, a workhouse guard. (We were obliged to bring the suits against individuals, as we could not in the law sue the Government.) The suits were brought in no spirit of revenge, but merely that the Administration should not be allowed to forget its record of brutality, unless it chose to amend its conduct by passing the amendment. The suits were brought by the women who suffered the greatest abuse during the "night of terror" at the workhouse.

The Woman's Party conference came to a dramatic close during that first week in December with an enormous mass meeting to honor those who had been arrested. The Belasco Theatre was packed to the rafters, with thousands more outside literally storming the building in their eagerness to be part of the event. Inside there was a fever heat of enthusiasm, bursting cheers, and thundering applause which shook the building. America has never before nor since seen such a suffrage meeting.

Mrs. Belmont, chairman, opened the meeting by saying:

> We are here this afternoon to do honor to a hundred gallant women, who have endured the hardship and humiliation of imprisonment because they love liberty.
>
> The suffrage pickets stood at the White House gates for ten months and dramatized the women's agitation for political liberty.

Self-respecting and patriotic American women will no longer tolerate a government which denies women the right to govern themselves. A flame of rebellion is abroad among women, and the stupidity and brutality of the government in this revolt have only served to increase its heat....

While the Government has endeavored to parry, tire, divert, and cheat us of our goal, the country has risen in protest against this evasive policy of suppression until today the indomitable pickets with their historic legends stand triumphant before the nation.

Mrs. William Kent, who had led the last picket line of forty-one women, was chosen to decorate the prisoners. "In honoring these women, who were willing to go to jail for liberty, we are showing our love of country and devotion to democracy."

The long line of prisoners filed past her and, amidst constant cheers and applause, received a tiny silver pin, a replica of a prison cell door bound by a delicate chain and heart-shaped lock. It was a badge of courage given to those who had been jailed for freedom.

As proof of this admiration for what the women had done, the great audience in a very few moments pledged $86,326 to continue the campaign. Imperative resolutions calling upon President Wilson and his Administration to act were unanimously passed amid the glorious uproar.

CHAPTER FIFTEEN

Political Results

IMMEDIATELY FOLLOWING the release of the prisoners and the magnificent demonstration of public support of them, political events happened rapidly.

First, the Judiciary Committee of the House voted 18 to 2 to report the amendment to that body. The measure had been reported to the Senate in the closing days of the previous session and was therefore already before the Senate awaiting action.

To be sure, the Judiciary Committee reported the amendment without recommendation. But soon after the members of the Suffrage Committee were appointed, most of whom were in favor of national suffrage, the committee met and decided to take the suffrage measure out of the hands of the Judiciary Committee and to press for a vote in the House.

Representative Frank W. Mondell of Wyoming, Republican, declared that the Republican side of the House would give more than a two-thirds majority of its members to the amendment. "It is up to our friends on the Democratic side to see that the amendment is not defeated through hostility or indifference on their side," said Mr. Mondell.

Our daily poll of the House showed constant gains. Pledges from both Democratic and Republican members came quickly; cabinet members for the first time publicly declared their belief in the amendment. A final poll, however, showed that we lacked a few votes of the necessary two-thirds majority to pass the measure in the House. More pressure was put on the President to secure additional Democratic votes.

Finally, on the eve of the vote President Wilson made his first declaration of support of the amendment during a meeting with a committee of Democratic Congressmen in which he advised them "to vote for the amendment as an act of right and justice to the women of the country and of the world."

During the vote the following day, Representative James C. Cantrill of Kentucky spoke to the House:

> To my Democratic brethren who have made these halls ring with their eloquence in their pleas to stand by the President, I will say that now is your chance to stand by the President and vote for this amendment. Do you wish to do that which is right and just toward the women of your own country? If so, follow the President's advice and vote for this amendment. It will not do to follow the President in this great crisis in the world's history on those matters only which are popular in your own districts. The true test is to stand by him, even though your own vote is unpopular at home. In the end, right and justice will prevail everywhere.... No one thing connected with the war is of more importance at this time than meeting the reasonable demand of millions of patriotic women of the Nation that the amendment for woman suffrage be submitted to the States.

After lengthy and sometimes bitter debate, the amendment passed the House of Representatives on January 10, 1918, by a vote of 274 to 136—a two-thirds majority with one vote to spare—*exactly forty years to a day from the time the suffrage amendment was first introduced into Congress and exactly one year to a day from the time the first picket banner appeared at the gate of the White House.*

It is our firm belief that the solid year of picketing, with all its political ramifications, compelled the President to abandon his opposition and declare himself for the measure. I do not mean to say that many things do not cooperate in a movement toward a great event. I do mean to say that picketing was the most vital force amongst the elements which moved President Wilson. That picketing had compelled Congress to see the question in terms of political capital is also true.

From the first word uttered in the House debate until the final roll call, political expediency was the chief motif.

The resentment at having been forced by the pickets to pass the amendment was evident throughout the debate. Representative William Gordon of Ohio, a Democrat, said with bitterness:

> We are threatened by these militant suffragettes with a direct and lawless invasion by the Congress of the United States of the rights of those States which have refused to confer upon their women the privilege of voting. This attitude on the part of some of the suffrage members of this House is on an exact equality with the acts of these women militants who have spent the last summer and fall, while they were not in the District Jail or workhouse, coaxing, teasing, and nagging the President of the United States for the purpose of inducing him, by coercion, to club Congress into adopting this joint resolution.

Shouts of "Well, they got him!" and "They got it!" from all sides, followed by prolonged laughter and jeers, interrupted the flow of his oratory.

Mr. Scott Ferris of Oklahoma, Democrat, hoped to minimize the effectiveness of the picket:

> I do not approve or believe in picketing the White House, the National Capitol, or any other station to bring about votes for women. I do not approve of wild militancy, hunger strikes, and efforts of that sort. I do not approve of the course of those women that…become agitators, lay off their womanly qualities in their efforts to secure votes. I do not approve of anything unwomanly anywhere, any time, and my course today in supporting this suffrage amendment is not guided by such conduct on the part of a very few women here or elsewhere.

Representative John W. Langley of Kentucky, Republican, had a different view of the pickets:

> When passing up and down the Avenue I frequently witnessed cultured, intellectual women arrested and dragged off to prison

because of their method of giving publicity to what they believed to be the truth. I will confess that the question sometimes rose in my mind whether, when the impartial history of this great struggle has been written, their names may not be placed upon the roll of martyrs to the cause to which they were consecrating their lives in the manner that they deemed most effective.

And so the debate went on. Occasionally one caught a glimmer of real comprehension among these men who were about to vote on our political liberty, but more often the discussion stayed on a very inferior level.

Even supporters of the measure had difficulty not to romanticize about "woman—God's noblest creation"…"man's better counterpart"…"humanity's perennial hope"…"the world's object most to be admired and loved"…and so forth.

Said Mr. Edward W. Gray of New Jersey, Republican:

> A nation will endure just so long as its men are virile. History, physiology and psychology all show that giving woman equal political rights with man makes ultimately for the deterioration of manhood. It is, therefore, not only because I want our country to win this war but because I want our nation to possess the male virility necessary to guarantee its future existence that I am opposed to the pending amendment.

Mr. James H. Mays of Utah was one Democrat who placed the responsibility for militancy where it rightly belonged when he said: "Some say today that they are ashamed of the action of militants in picketing the Capitol…. But we should be more ashamed of the unreasonable stubbornness on the part of the men who refused them the justice they have so long and patiently asked."

After a lengthy debate, the House finally passed the national suffrage amendment. We now turned our attention to the Senate.

Chapter Sixteen

An Interlude
of Seven Months

THE PRESIDENT had finally thrown his power to putting the amendment through the House. We hoped he would follow this up by insisting upon the passage of the amendment in the Senate. We ceased our acts of dramatic protest for the moment and gave our energies to getting public pressure upon him, to persuade him to see that the Senate acted. We also continued to press directly upon recalcitrant Senators of the minority party who could be won only through appeals other than from the President.

There are in the Senate ninety-six members—two elected from each of the forty-eight states. To pass a constitutional amendment through the Senate, sixty-four votes are necessary, a two-thirds majority. At this point in the campaign, fifty-three Senators were pledged to support the measure and forty-three were opposed. We still had to win eleven more votes. A measure passed through one branch of Congress must be passed through the other branch during the life of that Congress, otherwise it dies automatically and must be born again in a new Congress. We therefore had only the remainder of the first regular session of the Sixty-fifth Congress and, failing of that, the short second session from December 1918 to March 1919, in which to win those votes.

Organized demand for action grew to huge proportions in the states of the Senators not yet committed to the amendment. We turned also to the leading influential members of the respective parties for their help, asking them to state publicly their support of the amendment.

Former President Theodore Roosevelt did his most effective suffrage work at this period in a determined attack upon the few unconvinced Republican Senators. He was one of the few leaders in our national life who was never too busy to confer or to offer and accept suggestions as to procedure. He never took a patronizing attitude nor did he dogmatically tell you how the fight should be waged and won. He presupposed ability among women leaders. He was not offended, morally or politically, by our preferring to go to jail rather than to submit in silence. His sagacious attitude toward conservative and radical suffrage forces was always delightful and indicative of his appreciation of the political and social value of a movement's having vitality enough to disagree on methods.

When Mr. Roosevelt made a public statement in which he pointed to the superior support of the Republicans and urged even more liberal party support to ensure the passage of the amendment in the Senate, action by the opposing party followed quickly. In response, the National Executive Committee of the Democratic party passed a resolution calling for favorable action on the suffrage amendment in the Senate.

Republican and Democratic state, county and city committees then all called for Senate action. Several state legislatures demanded the Senate pass the measure, that they in turn might immediately ratify the amendment.

I was at this time Chairman of the Political Department of the Woman's Party, and in that capacity interviewed practically every national leader in both majority parties. Some supported our cause while others did not. Following are some of their comments:

Colonel William Boyce Thompson of New York, now Chairman of Ways and Means of the Republican National Committee, contributed ten thousand dollars to the campaign "for the passage of the suffrage amendment through the Senate, one hundred dollars for each of the pickets who went to prison because she stood at the gates of the White House, asking for the passage of the suffrage measure."

Former President William Howard Taft, then joint Chairman of the National Labor Board, declined to support "a proposition which adds more voters to our electorate.... The trouble in this country is we've got too many *men* voting as it is. Why, I'd take the vote away from most of the men."

Herbert Hoover, Chief Food Administrator, was not willing to say a single word on behalf of the political liberty of women. He sent word through his secretary that he could give no consideration to the suffrage question until the war was over. Mr. Hoover was the only important man in public life who steadfastly refused to see our representatives. (Later, after announcing his candidacy for nomination to the presidency, he authorized his secretary to write us a letter saying he had always been for woman suffrage.)

Mr. Bainbridge Colby, then member of the Emergency Fleet Corporation and now Secretary of State, told us, "In the light of world events, this reform is insignificant. No time or energy ought to be diverted from the great program of crushing the Germans."

Bernard Baruch, then member of the Council of National Defense and later economic expert at the Peace Conference, was able to see the war and the women's problems at the same time. He saw the passage of the amendment as a political asset and he agreed to tell the President that he believed it wise to put more pressure on the measure in the Senate.

William Randolph Hearst in powerful newspaper editorials called upon the Senators to act. I must say that the great majority of public men did offer help at this critical juncture.

Our pressure from below and that of the leaders from above began to have its effect. An attempt was made by Administration leaders to force a vote on May 19, 1918, but friends interceded when it was shown that not enough votes were pledged to secure passage. Again the vote was tentatively set for June 27 and again postponed.

Still unwilling to believe that we would be forced to resume our militancy, we attempted to talk to the President again. A special deputation of women munition workers was sent to him under the auspices of the Woman's Party. The women waited for a week, hoping he would consent to see them. "No time," was the answer. So the munition workers were forced to submit their appeal in writing. "We are only a few of the thousands of American women who are forming a growing part of the army at home. The work we are doing is hard and dangerous to life and health, making detonators, handling TNT, the highest of all explosives. We want to be recognized by our country, as much her citizens as our soldiers are." The President responded that he was doing everything that he could do in behalf of the suffrage amendment.

When an opportunity was given the President to show his sympathy for a world-wide endeavor just after having ignored our pleas at home, he hastened to accept. In response to a memorial transmitted through Carrie Chapman Catt, President of the International Woman Suffrage Alliance, the French Union for Woman Suffrage urged the President to use his aid on their behalf "which will be a powerful influence for woman suffrage in the entire world." The memorial was endorsed by the suffrage committees of Great Britain, Italy, Belgium and Portugal. The President took the occasion to say: "The democratic reconstruction of the world will not have been completely or adequately obtained until women are admitted to the suffrage. As for America, it is my earnest hope that the Senate of the United States will give an unmistakable answer by passing the federal amendment before the end of this session."

As a result, four more Democratic Senators pledged their support to the amendment, influenced both by the President's declaration of support and by widespread demands from their constituents at home. During this same period the Republican side of the Senate gave five more Republican Senators to the amendment. All of these men except for Senator Porter J. McCumber, were won through the pressure from Republican Party leaders. (Senator McCumber, though opposed, was compelled to support the measure by action of the North Dakota legislature commanding him to do so.) Only two votes remained to be won.

When, at the end of seven months from the time the amendment had passed the House, we still lacked these two votes, and the President gave no guarantee that he would put forth sufficient effort to secure them, we felt compelled to renew our attacks upon the President.

CHAPTER SEVENTEEN

New Attacks on the President

THE SENATE was about to recess. No assurance was given by the Democrats that suffrage would be considered either before or after the recess. Alarmed and aroused, we decided upon a national protest in Washington August 6, 1918, the anniversary of the birth of Inez Milholland (Boissevain).

Our protest took the form of a meeting at the base of the Lafayette Monument in the park directly opposite the White House. Nearly one hundred women from many States in the Union, dressed in white, marched from Headquarters to the monument carrying banners of purple, white and gold, led by a standard-bearer carrying the American flag. They made a beautiful mass of color as they grouped themselves around the statue. One banner bore Inez Milholland's memorable last words:

HOW LONG MUST WOMEN WAIT FOR LIBERTY?

Another banner carried the message of the meeting:

WE PROTEST AGAINST THE CONTINUED DISENFRANCHISE-MENT OF AMERICAN WOMEN, FOR WHICH THE PRESIDENT OF THE UNITED STATES IS RESPONSIBLE. WE DEMAND THAT THE PRESIDENT AND HIS PARTY SECURE THE PAS-SAGE OF THE SUFFRAGE AMENDMENT THROUGH THE SENATE IN THE PRESENT SESSION.

Suffragists in a demonstration at Lafayette Monument, Washington, D.C., 1918.
(National Woman's Party)

Mrs. Lawrence Lewis of Philadelphia, the first speaker, began: "We are here because when our country is at war for liberty and democracy...." At that point she was roughly seized by a policeman and placed under arrest. The great audience stood in absolute and amazed silence.

Hazel Hunkins of Montana took her place. "Here at the statue of Lafayette, who fought for the liberty of this country," she began, "and under the American flag, I am asking for...." She too was immediately arrested.

Miss Vivian Pierce of California began: "President Wilson has said...." She was dragged to the waiting patrol car.

One after another came forward in an attempt to speak, but no one was allowed to continue. Wholesale arrests followed. Before the crowd could really appreciate what had happened, forty-eight women had been hustled to the police station by the wagon load, their gay banners floating from the backs of the somber patrol wagons. They were told that the police had arrested them under the orders of Colonel C. Ridley, the President's military aide. All were released on bail and ordered to appear in court the following day.

The next day they were informed by the Government's attorney that he would have to postpone the trial so that he might have time to examine witnesses to see "what offense, if any, the women would be charged with." "I cannot go on with this case," he said, "*I have had no orders*. There are no precedents for cases like these...."

The women demanded that their cases be dismissed, or else a charge made against them. They were merely told to return on the appointed day. Such was the indignation aroused against the Administration for taking this action that Senator Charles Curtis of Kansas, Republican whip, stated publicly:

> The truth of this statement is made evident by the admission of the court that the forty-eight suffragists are arrested upon absolutely no charges, and that these women, among them munition workers and Red Cross workers, are held in Washington until next Tuesday, under arrest, while the United States Attorney for the District of Columbia decides for what offense, "if any," they were arrested.
>
> The meeting was called to make a justified protest against continued blocking of the suffrage amendment by the Democratic majority in the Senate. It is well known that three-fourths of the Republican membership in the Senate are ready to vote for the amendment, but under the control of the Democratic majority the Senate has recessed for six weeks without making any provision for action on this important amendment. In justice to the women who have been working so hard for the amendment it should be passed at the earliest date.

When the women finally came to trial ten days after their arrest, to face the charge of "holding a meeting in public grounds," and for "climbing on a statue," the women answered the roll call but remained silent thereafter. The familiar farce ensued. Some were released for lack of identification. The others were sentenced to the District Jail—for ten days if they had merely assembled to hold a public meeting, for fifteen days if they had also climbed on a statue.

The Administration evidently hoped by lighter sentences to avoid a hunger strike by the prisoners.

The women were taken immediately to a building, formerly used as a man's workhouse, situated in the swamps of the District prison grounds. This building, which had been declared unfit for human habitation in 1909, and which had been uninhabited ever since, was now reopened to receive twenty-six women who had attempted to hold a meeting in a public park in Washington. The women protested in a body and demanded to be treated as political prisoners. This being refused, all save two very elderly women, too frail to do so, went on hunger strike at once.

This place was the worst the women had experienced. Hideous aspects which had not been encountered in the workhouse and jail were encountered here. The cells were damp and cold. The doors were partly of solid steel with only a small section of grating, so that a very tiny amount of light penetrated the cells. The cots were of iron, without any spring and with only a thin straw pallet to lie upon. So frightful were the nauseating odors which permeated the place, and so terrible was the drinking water from the disused pipes, that one prisoner after another became violently ill.

As a kind of relief from the revolting odors, the prisoners took their straw pallets from the cells to the floor outside. They were ordered back to their cells but refused in a body to go. They preferred the stone floors to the vile odors within.

Conditions were so shocking that when Senators began to visit their constituents in this terrible hole, many of them protested to the authorities. Protests came in from all over the country, too.

At the end of the fifth day the Administration succumbed to the hunger strike and released the prisoners, who were trembling with weakness, chills and fever, scarcely able even to walk to the ambulance or motor car.

Two days after the release of the women, the Republican Party, for the first time in the history of woman suffrage, caucused in the Senate

Suffragist prisoners on straw pallets on jail floor. (National Woman's Party)

Suffragist prisoner, Mrs. Lawrence (Dora) Lewis, released from jail after a hunger strike. (National Woman's Party)

in favor of forcing suffrage to a vote. The Republicans were proud of their suffrage strength. They knew the Democrats were not. With the Congressional elections approaching, the Republicans meant to do their part toward acquainting the country with the Administration's policy of vacillation and delay. This was not only helpful to the Republicans politically; it was also advantageous to the amendment in that it goaded the majority party into action.

Nine months had passed since the vote in the House and we were perilously near the end of the session. On September 16, Senator Lee Overman, Democrat, Chairman of the Rules Committee, told us that suffrage was "not on the program for this session" and that the Senate would recess in a few days for the election campaigns without considering any more legislation. On the same day Senator Jones, Chairman of the Suffrage Committee, announced to us that he would not even call his Committee together to consider taking a vote.

We had announced two weeks earlier that another protest meeting would be held at the base of the Lafayette Monument on that day, September 16, at four o'clock. No sooner had this protest been announced than the President publicly stated that he would receive a delegation of Southern and Western women partisans on the question of the amendment at *two* o'clock the same day.

To this delegation he said, "I am, as I think you know, heartily in sympathy with you. I have endeavored to assist you in every way in my power, and I shall continue to do so. I will do all I can to urge the passage of the amendment by an early vote."

Presumably this was expected to disarm us and perhaps silence our demonstration. However, it merely moved us to make another hasty visit to Senators Overman and Jones to see if the President's comments had altered their statements made earlier in the day.

These Administration leaders assured us that their statements stood; that no provision had been made for action on the amendment; that the President's statement did not mean that a vote would be taken this session; and that they did not contemplate being so advised by him.

Such a situation was intolerable. The President was uttering more fine words, while his Administration leaders interpreted them to mean nothing, but they were not followed by action on his part.

We therefore changed our planned demonstration to a more drastic form of protest. We took the very words the President spoke that afternoon to the base of Lafayette Monument and burned them in a flaming torch.

A throng had gathered to hear the speakers. Ceremonies were opened with the reading of the following appeal written by Mrs. Richard Wainwright, wife of Rear Admiral Wainwright:

> Lafayette, we are here! We, the women of the United States, denied the liberty which you helped to gain, and for which we have asked in vain for sixty years, turn to you to plead for us.
>
> As our army now in France spoke to you there, saying here we are to help your country fight for liberty, will you not speak here and now for us, a little band with no army, no power but justice and right, no strength but in our Constitution and in the Declaration of Independence; and win a great victory again in this country by giving us the opportunity we ask—to be heard through the Susan B. Anthony amendment. Lafayette, we are here!

Before the enthusiastic applause for Mrs. Wainwright's appeal had died away, Lucy Branham of Baltimore stepped forward with a flaming torch, which she applied to the President's latest words on suffrage. The police looked on and smiled, and the crowd cheered as she said:

> The torch which I hold symbolizes the burning indignation of the women who for years have been given words without action.... For five years women have appealed to this President and his party for political freedom. The President has given words, and words, and words. Today women receive more words. We announce to the President and the whole world today, by this act of ours, our determination that words shall no longer be the only reply given to American women—our determination that this same democracy for whose establishment abroad we are making the utmost sacrifice shall also prevail at home.
>
> We have protested to this Administration by banners; we have protested by speeches; we now protest by this symbolic act. As in

the ancient fights for liberty, the crusaders for freedom symbolized their protest against those responsible for injustice by consigning their hollow phrases to the flames, so we, on behalf of
thousands of suffragists, in this same way today protest against
the action of the President and his party in delaying the liberation of American women.

At this point a man in the crowd handed up a twenty-dollar bill for
the campaign in the Senate. This was the signal for others. Bills and
coins were passed up. Instantly marshals ran hither and thither collecting the money in improvised baskets while the cheers grew louder
and louder. Many of the policemen present were among the donors.

Burning President Wilson's words had met with popular approval
from this large and enthusiastic crowd!

The procession of women was starting back to Headquarters, the
police were eagerly clearing the way for the line; the crowd was dis-
persing in order; the great golden banner, MR. PRESIDENT, WHAT
WILL YOU DO FOR WOMAN SUFFRAGE? was just swinging past the
White House gate, when President Wilson stepped into his car for his
afternoon drive.

CHAPTER EIGHTEEN

President Wilson
Appeals to the Senate

THE NEXT DAY the Administration completely reversed its policy. Senator Andrieus A. Jones, Chairman of the Suffrage Committee, announced that the suffrage amendment would be considered in the Senate on September 26. And Senator Lee Overman, Chairman of the Rules Committee, reversed himself and told us that he had been mistaken yesterday and that the amendment was "now in the legislative program." With this promise of action, we immediately ceased our demonstrations, although we knew there were still two votes lacking to ensure passage.

The debate on September 26 opened with a long and eloquent speech in support of the amendment by Senator James K. Vardaman of Mississippi, Democrat. He was followed by another who attempted to explain why, although opposed to suffrage, he would vote for the amendment. An anti-suffrage Republican stated flatly, "that all questions involving declarations of war and terms of peace should be left to that sex which must do the fighting and the dying on the battlefield." One Senator said he considered woman as superior to man, and therefore could not trust her with a vote. And so it went.

The real excitement only began when Senator Key Pittman of Nevada, Democrat, attempted to reveal to the Senators of his party the actual seriousness of the political crisis in which the Democrats were now involved. He also tried to shift the blame for threatened defeat of the amendment to the Republican side of the chamber. There was a note of desperation in his voice, too, since he knew that President Wilson had not up to that moment won the two votes lacking.

"If we refer the amendment back to the Committee, then we will be charged, as we have been all the time in the suffrage States, with trying to prevent a vote on it, and still the Woman's Party campaign will go on as it is going on now; and if we vote on it they will say: 'We told you the Democrats would kill it, because the President would not make thirty-two on his side vote for it.'"

That was the crux of the whole situation. The Democrats had been maneuvered into a position where they could neither afford to move to refer the amendment back to the Committee, nor could they afford to press it to a losing vote. They were indeed in an exceedingly embarrassing predicament.

After days of debate the Senate adjourned, leaving things from the point of view of party politics, tangled in a hopeless knot. Then the excited word went out that the President would address the Senate on behalf of the amendment. It was his attempt to untie the knot. He said:

> I regard the concurrence of the Senate in the constitutional amendment proposing the extension of the suffrage to women as vitally essential to the successful prosecution of the great war of humanity in which we are engaged. I have come to urge upon you the considerations which have led me to that conclusion....
> It is my duty to win the war and to ask you to remove every obstacle that stands in the way of winning it.
>
> If we be indeed democrats and wish to lead the world to democracy, we can ask other peoples to accept in proof of our sincerity and our ability to lead them whither they wish to be led nothing less persuasive and convincing than our actions. They are looking to the great, powerful, famous democracy of the West to lead them to the new day for which they have so long waited; and they think, in their logical simplicity, that democracy means that women shall play their part in affairs alongside men and upon an equal footing with them. If we reject measures like

this, in ignorance or defiance of what a new age has brought forth, they will cease to follow or to trust us....

Are we alone to refuse to learn the lesson? Are we alone to ask and take the utmost that women can give—service and sacrifice of every kind—and still say that we do not see what title that gives them to stand by our sides in the guidance of the affairs of their nation and ours? We have made partners of the women in this war; shall we admit them only to a partnership of sacrifice and suffering and toil and not to a partnership of privilege and of right? This war could not have been fought, either by the other nations engaged or by America, if it had not been for the services of the women.... We shall not only be distrusted but shall deserve to be distrusted if we do not enfranchise them with the fullest possible enfranchisement, as it is now certain that the other great free nations will enfranchise them.

The women of America are too noble and too intelligent and too devoted to be slackers whether you give or withhold this thing that is mere justice; but I know the magic it will work in their thoughts and spirits if you give it them. I propose it as I would propose to admit soldiers to the suffrage, the men fighting in the field for our liberties and the liberties of the world, were they excluded. The tasks of the women lie at the very heart of the war, and I know how much stronger that heart will beat if you do this just thing and show our women that you trust them as much as you in fact and of necessity depend upon them....

I tell you plainly, as commander-in-chief of our armies and of the gallant men in our fleets, as the present spokesman of this people in our dealings with the men and women throughout the world who are now our partners, as the responsible head of a great government...as the guide and director of forces caught in the grip of war and by the same token in need of every material and spiritual resource this great nation possesses, I tell you plainly that this measure is vital to the winning of the war and to the energies alike of preparation and of battle.

And not to the winning of the war only. It is vital to the right solution of the great problems which we must settle, and settle immediately, when the war is over.... The problems of that time will strike to the roots of many things...and I for one believe that our safety in those questioning days will depend upon the direct and authoritative participation of women in our counsels. We shall need their moral sense to preserve what is right and fine and worthy in our system of life as well as to discover just what it is that ought to be purified and reformed. Without their counselings we shall be only half wise.

That is my case. This is my appeal. Many may deny its validity, if they choose, but no one can brush aside or answer the arguments upon which it is based. The executive tasks of this war rest upon me. I ask that you lighten them and place in my hands instruments, spiritual instruments, which I do not now possess, which I sorely need, and which I have daily to apologize for not being able to employ.

It was a truly beautiful and memorable appeal.

When the applause and the excitement accompanying a message from the President had subsided, and the floor of the chamber had emptied itself of its distinguished visitors, the debate resumed.

Then, finally, the time had come to take the vote, but we knew we had not won. The roll was called and the vote, on October 1, 1918, stood 62 to 34. We had lost by two votes.

Instantly Chairman Jones, according to his promise to the women, changed his vote from "yes" to "nay," which allowed him to move for a reconsideration of the measure and thus automatically keep it on the calendar of the Senate. That was all that could be done.

The President's belief in the power of words had lost the amendment. His speech, eloquent as it was, could not break down the opposition in the Senate which he had so long protected and condoned.

Chapter Nineteen

More Pressure

OUR IMMEDIATE TASK was to compel the President to secure a reversal of two votes in the Senate. We decided to modify our tactics slightly and to enter again the Congressional elections which were a month away.

There were two senatorial contests coming up—in New Jersey and New Hampshire—to fill vacancies caused by death. That gave us an opportunity to elect two pro-suffrage friends who would take their seats in time to vote on the amendment before the end of this session. It so happened that the Democratic candidates were pledged to vote for the amendment if elected, and that the Republican candidates were opposed to the amendment. And so we launched our campaign for the election of the two Democratic candidates.

We went immediately to the President to ask his assistance in our endeavor. We urged him personally to appeal to the voters of New Jersey and New Hampshire on behalf of these two candidates. Both of the candidates themselves appealed to President Wilson for help in their contests, on the basis of their suffrage advocacy. His speech to the Senate scarcely cold, the President refused to lend any assistance in these contests, which with sufficient effort might have produced the last two votes.

At the end of two weeks of such pressure, it was clear that the President would move again only under attack. We went again, therefore, to the women voters of the West and asked them to withhold their support from the Democratic Senatorial candidates in the suffrage States in order to compel the President to assist in the two Eastern contests.

This campaign made it clear to the President that we were still holding him and his party responsible for the passage of the amendment.

Our policy, as before, was to oppose the Democratic candidates at elections so long as their party did not pass the amendment. Since there was no question between individuals in suffrage States—they are all suffragists—this could not change our numerical strength. It could, however, demonstrate the growing and comprehensive power of the women voters.

Throughout the election campaign, we also attempted to hold banners at the Capitol in order to weaken the resistance of the Senators of the opposition. The mottoes on the banners attacked with impartial mercilessness both Democrats and Republicans. One read:

> GERMANY HAS ESTABLISHED "EQUAL, UNIVERSAL, SECRET, DIRECT FRANCHISE." THE SENATE HAS DENIED EQUAL, UNIVERSAL, SECRET SUFFRAGE TO AMERICA. WHICH IS MORE OF A DEMOCRACY, GERMANY OR AMERICA?

On the first day of picketing, as the women approached the Senate, Colonel Higgins, the Sergeant at Arms of the Senate, ordered a squad of Capitol policemen to rush upon them. The banners were wrenched from their hands and the women were taken into the guardroom where they were detained for varying periods of time. When the women insisted on knowing upon what charges they were held, they were merely told that "peace and order must be maintained on the Capitol grounds," and further, it made no difference about the law, as Colonel Higgins had taken the law in his own hands.

Day after day this performance went on. Small detachments of women attempted to hold banners outside the United States Senate. Instead of maintaining peace and order, the squads of police managed to keep the Capitol grounds in a state of confusion. They were sometimes assisted by Senate pages, small errand boys who would run out and attack the women with impunity. Each day the women would be held until the Senate had safely adjourned. The next day the whole spectacle would be repeated.

Shortly before the election, when our campaign was in full swing in the West, the President finally appealed to the voters of New Jersey and New Hampshire to elect the Democratic candidates for Senator. However, we continued our campaign in the West as a safeguard against relaxation by the President after his appeal. There were seven senatorial contests in the Western suffrage States. In all but two of these contests the Democratic senatorial candidates were defeated.

Despite the President's appeal, Republicans won in New Jersey and New Hampshire. Throughout the country, Republicans were elected to the extent that they would hold a majority in Congress when the new session began the following year. Meanwhile, world events rushed on. German autocracy had collapsed. The Allies had won a military victory. The Kaiser had fled for his life because of the uprising of his people. The Great War came to an end.

"We are all free voters of a free republic now," was the message sent by the women of Germany to the women of the United States through Miss Jane Addams. We were at that moment heartily ashamed of our Government. German women voting, while American women were going to jail and spending long hours in the Senate guardhouse without arrests or charges.

When the Sixty-fifth Congress reconvened for its short and final session on December 2, 1918 (less than a month after our election campaign), President Wilson, for the first time, included suffrage in his regular message to Congress, the very thing that we had asked of him at the opening of every session of Congress since March 1913.

There were now fewer than a hundred days in which to get action from the Senate and to avoid losing the benefit of our victory in the House. In his opening address to Congress, the President again appealed to the Senate in these words:

> And what shall we say of the women—of their instant intelligence, quickening every task that they touched; their capacity for organization and cooperation, which gave their action discipline and enhanced the effectiveness of everything they attempted; their aptitude at tasks to which they had never before set their hands; their utter self-sacrifice alike in what they did and in what they gave? Their contribution to the great result is beyond appraisal. They have added a new luster to the annals of American womanhood.

The least tribute we can pay them is to make them the equals of men in political rights, as they have proved themselves their equals in every field of practical work they have entered, whether for themselves or for their country. These great days of completed achievement would be sadly marred were we to omit that act of justice. Besides the immense practical services they have rendered, the women of the country have been the moving spirits in the systematic economics in which our people have voluntarily assisted to supply the suffering peoples of the world and the armies upon every front with food and everything else we had, that might serve the common cause. The details of such a story can never be fully written but we carry them at our hearts and thank God that we can say that we are the kinsmen of such.

Again we looked for action to follow this appeal. Again we found that the President had uttered these words but had made no plan to translate them into action.

And so his second appeal to the Senate failed. He could not overcome with additional eloquence the opposition which he himself had so long formulated, defended, encouraged and solidified, especially when that eloquence was followed by either no action or only half-hearted efforts.

It would now require a determined assertion of his political power as the leader of his party. We would make a final appeal to him to demand the necessary two votes to pass the amendment in the Senate.

Chapter Twenty

The President
Sails Away

N O SOONER had we set ourselves to a brief, hot campaign to compel President Wilson to win the final votes than he sailed away to France to attend the Peace Conference at the end of the World War, sailed away to consecrate himself to liberating the oppressed peoples of the whole world. He cannot be condemned for aiming to achieve so gigantic a task. But we reflected that again the President had refused his specific aid in our humble aspirations for liberty at home.

We knew it was positively impossible for us, by our own efforts, to win the last two votes. Only pressure from the President could win them. It was true that he had left his message urging the Senate to act, but it is also true that Administration leaders did not consider these words a command. It must be realized that even after the President had been compelled to declare publicly his support of the measure, it was almost impossible to get his own leaders to take seriously his words on suffrage. And so again the Democratic Chairman of the Senate Rules Committee had no thought of bringing the amendment to a vote. The Democratic Chairman of the Woman Suffrage Committee assumed not the slightest responsibility for its success, nor could he produce any plan whereby the last votes could be won. They knew, as well as did we, that only the President could win those last two votes. They made it perfectly clear that until he had done so, they could do nothing.

Less than fifty legislative days remained to us before Congress adjourned. Something had to be done quickly, something bold and offensive enough to threaten the prestige of the President as champion of world liberty; something which might penetrate his reverie and shock him into concrete action. This was the feeling of the four hundred officers of the National Woman's Party, summoned to a three-day conference in Washington in December 1918. It was unanimously decided to stage a dramatic event in which we would light a fire in an urn, and, on the day that the President was officially received by France, burn with fitting public ceremonies all the President's past and present speeches or books concerning "liberty," "freedom" and "democracy."

It was late afternoon on December 16 when hundreds of women proceeded solemnly in single file from Headquarters, past the White House, along the edge of the quiet and beautiful Lafayette Park, to the foot of Lafayette's statue. A slight mist was falling. Half the women carried lighted torches, the other half carried purple, white and gold banners. A crowd gathered silently, somewhat awe-struck by the scene. Massed about that statue, we felt a strange strength and solidarity, we felt again that we were a part of the universal struggle for liberty.

The torch was applied to the pine logs in the Grecian urn placed on the broad base of the statue. As the flames began to mount, Vida Milholland stepped forward and sang the "Woman's Marseillaise."

Mrs. John Rogers, Jr., chairman of the National Advisory Council, spoke:

> We hold this meeting to protest against the denial of liberty to American women. All over the world today we see surging and sweeping irresistibly on, the great tide of democracy, and women would be derelict in their duty if they did not see to it that it brings freedom to the women of this land....
>
> Our ceremony today is planned to call attention to the fact that President Wilson has gone abroad to establish democracy in foreign lands when he has failed to establish democracy at home. We burn his words on liberty today, not in malice or anger, but in a spirit of reverence for truth.

This meeting is a message to President Wilson. We expect an answer. If the answer is more words we will burn them again. The only answer the National Woman's Party will accept is the instant passage of the amendment in the Senate.

The few hoots and jeers which followed all ceased when a tiny and aged woman stepped forward to the urn. It was the most dramatic moment in the ceremony. Reverend Olympia Brown of Wisconsin, one of the first ordained women ministers in the country, then eighty-four years old, gallant pioneer, friend and colleague of Susan B. Anthony, said, as she threw into the flames the speech made by the President on his arrival in France: "I have fought for liberty for seventy years, and I protest against the President's leaving our country with this old fight here unwon."

Suffragists march to Lafayette Monument, Washington, D.C., to burn President Wilson's speeches. *(National Woman's Party)*

The crowd burst into applause and continued to cheer as she was assisted down from the base of the statue, too frail to dismount by herself. Then came the other representative women, from Massachusetts to California, from Georgia to Michigan, each one consigning to the flames various speeches of the President on freedom. The flames burned brighter and brighter as the night grew black.

The long line of bright torches shone menacingly as the women marched slowly back to Headquarters, and the crowd dispersed in silence. The White House was empty, but we knew our message would be heard in France.

CHAPTER TWENTY-ONE

Watchfires of Freedom

DECEMBER CAME to an end with no plan for action on the amendment assured. This left us January and February only before the session would end. The President had not yet won the necessary two votes. We decided therefore to keep a perpetual fire to consume the President's speeches on democracy as fast as he made them in Europe.

And so on New Year's Day 1919, we lit our first watchfire of freedom in the urn and placed it on the sidewalk in a direct line with the President's front door. The wood came from a tree in Independence Square, Philadelphia. Women with banners stood guard over the watchfire. A bell hung in the balcony at Headquarters tolled rhythmically the beginning of the watch. It rang again as the President's words were tossed to the flames. His speech to the workingmen of Manchester; his toast to the King at Buckingham Palace; his speech at Brest; all turned into ignominious brown ashes.

The bell tolled again when the watch was changed. All Washington was reminded hourly that we were at the President's gate, burning his words. From Washington the news went to all the world.

People gathered to see the ceremony. The omnipresent small boys and soldiers jeered, and some tore at the banners. A soldier rushed to the scene with a bucket of water to extinguish the flames, but the fire continued to burn as if by magic. A policeman used a fire extinguisher, but the fire burned on. The flames were as indomitable as the women who guarded them. Rain came, but all through the night the watchfire burned. All through the night the women stood guard.

Day and night the fire burned. Boys scattered it in the street, broke the urn, and destroyed the banners, but each time the women rekindled the fire. A squad of policemen tried to demolish the fire, but while the police were engaged at the White House gates, other women went quietly in the dusk to the huge bronze urn in Lafayette Park and lit another watchfire. The police hastened to the park and overturned the burning contents. Alice Paul refilled the urn and kindled a new fire. She was placed under arrest. Suddenly a third blaze was seen in a remote corner of the park. The policemen scrambled to extinguish it.

When the watchfires had been burning for four days and four nights, in spite of the attempts by the police to extinguish them, general orders to arrest the women were sent to the squad of policemen.

Five women were taken to the police station but were released without bail, since no one was able to supply a charge. Research later produced an ancient statute that prohibits the building of fires in a public place in the District of Columbia between sunset and sunrise.

In a few days eleven women were brought to trial. The prosecuting attorney read with heavy pomposity the charge against the prisoners: "That on Pennsylvania Avenue, in the District of Columbia, they did aid and abet in setting fire to certain combustibles consisting of logs, paper, oil, etc. between the setting of the sun on the fifth day of January and the rising of the sun of the sixth day of January 1919."

After brief testimony by the policemen, the judge found the prisoners "guilty" and required them to pay a fine of five dollars or serve five days in jail. The Administration evidently feared more hunger strikes and sought safety in lighter sentences. The judge pleaded with the women not to go to jail at all, offering probation if they would promise to be good and not light any more fires in the District of Columbia. The prisoners would make no such promise and were taken to jail where they straightway started a hunger strike.

Meanwhile the watchfires continued in the Capital. January 13, the day the great world Peace Conference under the President's leadership began to deliberate on the task of administering "right" and "justice" to all the oppressed of the earth, twenty-three women were arrested in front of the White House. Another trial and more women were sentenced to five days' imprisonment for lighting watchfires.

On January 25, in Paris, President Wilson received a delegation of French working women who urged woman suffrage as one of the points to be settled at the Peace Conference. The President expressed admiration for the women of France and told them of his deep personal interest in the enfranchisement of women. It was a great moment for the President. He had won the position in the eyes of the world of a devout champion of the liberty of women, but at the very moment he was speaking to these French women, American women were lying in the District of Columbia jail for demanding liberty at his gates.

When Mary Nolan, the eldest suffrage prisoner, took to the watchfire those words of the President to the French women, she too was arrested. The flames were just consuming the words, "All sons of freedom are under oath to see that freedom never suffers," when a whole squadron of police dashed up. There was a pause when they saw her age, but she was quickly marched off, amidst cheers from the

Guarding the watchfire in front of the White House. (National Woman's Party)

friendly crowd. During the women's trials, those who applauded their support and would not cease were also sentenced to jail for contempt of court.

And so, throughout January and the beginning of February 1919, the story of protest continued relentlessly. Watchfires—arrests—convictions—hunger strikes—release—until again the nation rose in protest against imprisoning the women and against the Senate's delay. Cables were sent to the President at the Peace Conference, demanding him to act. News of our demonstrations had also been well reported in the Paris press.

The situation must have seemed serious to him for, despite his reluctance, he did begin to cable Senate leaders, who in turn began to act. On February 2, the Democratic Suffrage Senators met. The next day Senator Jones announced in the Senate that the amendment would be brought up for discussion February 10. The following evening, a caucus of all Democratic Senators was called, the first Democratic caucus held in the Senate since war was declared.

Several hours of very passionate debate occurred, during which Senator William P. Pollock of South Carolina announced for the first time his support of the measure. He had yielded to pressure by cable from the President as well as to the caucus. Now only one vote was lacking.

Many Democratic leaders began to be alarmed that the last vote might not be secured. They enlisted William Jennings Bryan to speak to the Democratic opponents of the amendment in an attempt to gain support:

> Woman suffrage is coming to the country and to the world. It will be submitted to the States by the next Congress if it is not submitted by the present Congress. I hope the Democrats of the South will not handicap the Democrats of the North by compelling them to spend the next twenty-five years explaining to the women of the country why their party prevented the submission of the suffrage amendment to the States.
>
> This is our last chance to play an important part in bringing about this important reform, and it is of vital political concern

that the Democrats of the Northern Mississippi Valley should not be burdened by the charge that our party prevented the passage of the suffrage amendment, especially when it is known that it is coming in spite of, if not with the aid of, the Democratic Party.

As we grew nearer the last vote, the President was meeting what was perhaps his most bitter resistance from within. It was a situation which he could have prevented. His own early hostility to national suffrage, his later indifference and negligence, his actual protection given to Democratic opponents of the measure, his own reversal of policy only under pressure, the half-hearted efforts made by him on its behalf, were all coming to fruition at the moment when his continued prestige was at stake. His power to get results on the amendment was thus greatly weakened, and the opponents presented formidable resistance.

The watchfires continued.

Chapter Twenty-Two

Burned in Effigy

THE SUFFRAGE SCORE now stood as follows: One vote lacking in the Senate, fifteen days in which to win it, and President Wilson across the sea in Paris. The Democrats set February 10 as the date on which the Senate would again vote on the amendment, but they had no plan as to how the last vote would be won.

We were powerless to secure the last vote on our own. That was still the President's problem. Knowing that he always put forth more effort when under fire of protest from us, we decided to make, as a climax to our watchfire demonstrations, a more drastic form of protest. We wanted to show our contempt for the President's inadequate support which promised so much in words and which did so little in deeds.

And so on the day preceding the vote we planned to burn in effigy a portrait of President Wilson even as the Revolutionary Fathers in Delaware had burned a portrait of King George the day after the adoption of the Declaration of Independence.

One hundred women marched with banners to the center of the sidewalk opposite the White House. Mingling with the party's tricolored banners were two lettered ones which read:

ONLY FIFTEEN LEGISLATIVE DAYS ARE LEFT IN THIS CONGRESS. FOR MORE THAN A YEAR THE PRESIDENT'S PARTY HAS BLOCKED SUFFRAGE IN THE SENATE. IT IS BLOCKING IT TODAY. THE PRESIDENT IS RESPONSIBLE FOR THE BETRAYAL OF AMERICAN WOMANHOOD.

And:

WHY DOES NOT THE PRESIDENT INSURE THE PASSAGE OF SUF-
FRAGE IN THE SENATE TOMORROW? WHY DOES HE NOT WIN
FROM HIS PARTY THE ONE VOTE NEEDED? HAS HE AGREED TO
PERMIT SUFFRAGE AGAIN TO BE PUSHED ASIDE? PRESIDENT WIL-
SON IS DECEIVING THE WORLD. HE PREACHES DEMOCRACY
ABROAD AND THWARTS DEMOCRACY HERE.

As the marchers massed their banners and grouped themselves
about the urn, thousands of people closed in about them, a crowd so
enthralled that it stood almost motionless for two hours while the ceremonies continued. After the fire was kindled in the urn and the
flames leapt into the air, a figure of President Wilson sketched on
paper in black and white was dropped into the fire in the urn as a
symbol of our contempt.

Mrs. Henry O. Havemeyer of New York then said: "Every Anglo-
Saxon government in the world has enfranchised its women. In Russia, in Hungary, in Austria, in Germany itself, the women are completely enfranchised. We women of America are assembled here today
to voice our deep indignation that...American women are still
deprived of a voice in their Government at home. We mean to show
that the President...."

At that moment a policeman caught her by the arm, placed her
under arrest, and forced her into the waiting patrol wagon.

Thereupon the police fell upon the ceremonies, and indiscriminate
arrests followed. Women with banners were taken; women without
banners were taken. Women attempting to guard the fire; women
standing by doing nothing at all; all were seized and rushed to the
patrol. While this uproar was going on, others attempted to continue
Mrs. Havemeyer's speech, but each was apprehended. When the
patrol wagons were all filled to capacity, nearby automobiles were
commandeered, and more patrols summoned. And still not even half
the women were captured.

The police then suddenly ceased their raids and arrested no more.
Perhaps someone realized that a hundred additions to the already
overcrowded jail and workhouse would be too embarrassing. And so

the police turned their attention to the fascinated crowd, forcing back these masses of people half way across Pennsylvania Avenue and stationed an officer every two feet in front of them. Still women came to keep the fire burning. The police finally declared a "military zone" between the encircling crowd and the remaining women, and no person was allowed to enter the proscribed area. For another hour the women stood on guard at the urn, and as night fell, sixty of them marched back to Headquarters. Thirty-nine had been arrested.

The following morning, February 10, Senators gathered in the Senate Chamber to answer the roll call on the suffrage amendment. Every one knew that we still lacked one vote. The debate was confined to two speeches, one for and one against.

When the roll was called, sixty-three Senators voted in favor of the amendment, thirty-three against. The amendment lost by one vote. Of the sixty-three favorable votes, thirty-two were Republicans and thirty-one Democrats. Of the thirty-three adverse votes, twelve were Republicans and twenty-one Democrats. The amendment had been defeated by the opposition of the Democratic Administration and by the failure of the President to put behind it enough power to win.

Meanwhile, a few blocks away in the courthouse, thirty-nine women were being tried for their protest of the previous day. When twenty-six had been sentenced to prison, the judge wearily asked, "How many more are out there?" When told that he had tried only two-thirds of the defendants, he dismissed the remaining thirteen without trial! They were as guilty as their colleagues, but the judge was too tired to continue.

Senator Jones of New Mexico, Chairman of the Suffrage Committee, and his Democratic colleagues refused to reintroduce the Susan B. Anthony amendment in the Senate immediately after this defeat. But on Monday, February 17, the ranking Republican Senator on the Suffrage Committee obtained unanimous consent and reintroduced it, thereby placing it once more on its way to early reconsideration.

Our fight was not yet over.

CHAPTER TWENTY-THREE

Boston Militants
Welcome the President

PRESIDENT WILSON was scheduled to return to America from Europe on February 24, landing in Boston. That would leave seven days in which he could act to secure the final vote before Congress ended its session on March 3. We were determined to make another dramatic effort to move him further to aid our cause. Accordingly, Alice Paul went to Boston to arrange a demonstration.

We announced our plans in advance so the whole world would know that women were greeting President Wilson, why they were greeting him, and what form of demonstration the greetings would assume. Upon his arrival a line of silent pickets would hold banners calling for the President's aid. In the afternoon the women would gather in Boston Common and burn the parts of the President's Boston speech that pertained to democracy and liberty.

Boston officials reacted with almost unbelievable alarm. Prior to making our plans public, the front pages of the city's newspapers had been filled with the elaborate details for the welcome to be extended to the President, eulogies of the President, and recitals of his great triumph abroad. Now a large proportion of this space was devoted to the clever plans of the police to outwit the suffragists. They would establish a line in front of the reviewing stand beyond which no suffragist would be allowed to penetrate.

The day of the President's arrival came. Lines of marines were in formation to hold back the crowds from the reviewing stand where the President would appear after heading the procession in his honor. It seemed as if all Boston were on hand for the welcome. A slender file of twenty-two women marched silently into the sunshine, slipped through the established line and made its way to the base of the reviewing stand. There the women unfurled their banners, standing directly facing the line of marines which was supposed to keep all suffragists at bay. Quite calmly and yet triumphantly, they stood there, a pageant of beauty and defiant appeal.

Katherine Morey of Brookline held the American flag in the place of honor at the head of the line. On one side of the flag was the historic banner:

MR. PRESIDENT, HOW LONG MUST WOMEN WAIT FOR LIBERTY?

On the other side was a banner with the familiar words:

MR. PRESIDENT, WHAT WILL YOU DO FOR WOMAN SUFFRAGE?

A large lettered banner made especially for the occasion read:

MR. PRESIDENT, YOU SAID IN THE SENATE ON SEPTEMBER 20 "WE SHALL NOT ONLY BE DISTRUSTED BUT WE SHALL DESERVE TO BE DISTRUSTED IF WE DO NOT ENFRANCHISE WOMEN." YOU ALONE CAN REMOVE THIS DISTRUST BY SECURING THE ONE VOTE NEEDED TO PASS THE SUFFRAGE AMENDMENT BEFORE MARCH 4.

Other banners were simply purple, white and gold.

"When we had stood there about three quarters of an hour," said Katherine Morey later, "Superintendent of Police Crowley came to me and said, 'We want to be as nice as we can to you suffragette ladies, but you cannot stand here while the President goes by, so you might as well go back now.' I said I was sorry, but as we had come simply to be there at that very time, we would not be able to go back until the President had gone by. He thereupon made a final appeal to Miss Paul, who was at Headquarters, but she only repeated our statement."

The patrol wagons then hurried to the scene, and the women were arrested in an exceedingly gentlemanly manner. But the effect on the crowd was electric. The sight of women being put into police wagons seemed to thrill the Boston masses much more than anything the President subsequently said in his speech.

The women were taken to the House of Detention and charged with "loitering more than seven minutes." It was a most extraordinary situation. Thousands loitered from curiosity on the day the President arrived. Twenty-two loitered for liberty, and they were arrested.

That afternoon other women conducted a watchfire demonstration on Boston Common to continue to focus public attention upon our demand to the President. The ceremony began at three o'clock, presided over by Louise Sykes of Cambridge, whose late husband was President of the Connecticut College for Women. Throngs of people packed in closely in an effort to hear the speakers explain the purpose of the protest, the status of the amendment, and to urge those present to help. Mrs. Sykes then burned the words of the President's latest speech. At six o'clock three women were arrested and taken to the House of Detention, where they joined their comrades.

The House of Detention was characterized as a "dirty, filthy hole under the Court House." Katherine Morey described the situation: "We slept in our clothes, four women to a cell, on iron shelves two feet wide. In the cell was an open toilet. The place slowly filled up during the night with drunks and disorderlies until pandemonium reigned. In the evening, Superintendent Crowley and Commissioner Curtis came to call on us. I don't believe they had ever been there before, and they were painfully embarrassed. Superintendent Crowley said to me, 'If you were drunk we could release you in the morning, but unfortunately since you are not we have got to take you into court.'"

In the morning, when the prisoners were told that the Chief Justice had decided to try each prisoner separately and in closed court, they all protested. But guards took the women by force to a private room where the trial proceeded without the women's cooperation. "As an American citizen under arrest, I demand a public trial," was the statement of each on entering the judge's private trial room. Some were tried under wrong names, some were tried more than once under different names, but most of them under the name of Jane Doe.

Meanwhile, vigorous protests were being made to all the city officials by those supporters who had come to the court house to attend the trial. This protest was so strong that the last three women were finally tried in open court. The judge sentenced everybody impartially to eight days in jail in lieu of fines, with the exception of Miss Wilma Henderson, who was released when it was learned that she was a minor, and several others who could not be identified.

Sixteen women were taken to the Charles Street Jail to serve their sentences. The cells there were clean but lacked modern toilet facilities. The "toilet" consisted of a heavy wooden bucket, half filled with water that had to be carried to the lower floor—the women were on the third and fourth floor—every morning. A second bucket was provided for washing purposes.

The Boston newspaper reporters were admitted freely and they wrote columns of copy. Telegrams of protest from all over the country poured in upon all the Boston officials who had had any contact with the militant women. Telegrams also went from Boston, and especially from the jail, to President Wilson.

Official Boston was in the grip of this militant invasion when suddenly a man of mystery, one E. J. Howe, appeared and paid the women's fines on behalf of a "client." Whether he was acting for Boston officials, no one ever knew, but there were rumors that the city wished to end its embarrassment of jailing women.

The proper city of Boston had been profoundly shaken by these events. And as a result, its citizens gave more generously than ever before to militant suffrage finances. And when the "Prison Special," a special car of women prisoners that was touring the country, arrived in Boston a few days later their meeting hall was filled to overflowing with a crowd eager to hear more about their local heroines and to cheer them while they were decorated with the already famous prison pin.

CHAPTER TWENTY-FOUR

Democratic Congress Ends

IT WOULD BE FOLLY to say that President Wilson was not at this time aware of a very damning situation. Besides the events in Boston, the "Prison Special" was keeping public attention fixed upon the suffrage situation in the Senate. From coast to coast the prisoners were addressing enormous meetings and arousing thousands, especially in the South, to articulate condemnation of Administration tactics. It is impossible to calculate the number of cables which, as a result of this sensational tour, reached the President during his deliberations at the Peace Table in Paris or were waiting for him on his desk at the White House.

And so something happened in Washington after the President's return from Boston. He held a meeting with Senator Jones of New Mexico, Chairman of the Senate Suffrage Committee. As a result of this conference, Senator Jones introduced in the Senate on February 28 another resolution on suffrage. It was a little differently worded in that it gave the States the right to enforce the amendment with the provision that if they failed to do so, Congress would. This resolution was a concession to Senator Edward Gay of Louisiana, Democrat, who had voted against the measure on February 10, but who immediately pledged his vote in favor of the new resolution. Thus the sixty-fourth and last vote was won. But before the new resolution could be considered by Senate, unanimous consent was required.

On March 1 and two days following, Senator Jones attempted to get unanimous consent, but Republican anti-suffragists objected, blocking any action. And so the Sixty-fifth Congress with its Democratic majority ended on March 3, 1919, without passing the amendment.

On the face of it, Republicans had prevented action when the Democrats had finally secured the necessary votes. As a matter of fact, however, the President and his party were responsible. They waited until the last three days of the session to make the supreme effort. That the President did finally get the last vote even at a moment when parliamentary difficulties prevented it from being voted upon, proved our contention that he could pass the amendment at any time he set himself resolutely to it.

The fact that the majority of the Southern contingent in Wilson's party stood stubbornly against him on woman suffrage was, of course, a real obstacle, but we had seen the President overcome far greater obstacles. We had seen him lead a country—which had voted to stay out of the European war—into battle almost immediately after they had so voted. We had seen him conscript the men of the same stubborn South, which had been conspicuously opposed to conscription. We had seen him win mothers to his war point of view after they had fought passionately for him and his peace program at election time. In all these things he had taken pains to lead men and women—influential and obscure—to his way of thinking. And so we knew he was able to overcome obstacles when his heart and head were set to the task.

And since federal woman suffrage was neither in his head nor his heart, it had been our task to put it there. We had done our utmost.

For six full years, through three Congresses under President Wilson's power, the continual Democratic resistance, meandering, delays and deceits had left us still without the vote. A world war had come and gone during this span of effort. Vast millions had died in pursuit of liberty. A czar and a kaiser had been deposed. The Russian people had revolutionized their whole social and economic system. And here in the United States of America we couldn't even wrest from the leader of democracy and his associates the first step toward our political liberty—the passage of an amendment through Congress, which would submit the question of democracy to the states!

CHAPTER TWENTY-FIVE

A Farewell to President Wilson

IN NOVEMBER 1918 a Congress with a Republican majority had been elected, but it would not sit until December 1919—such was the system—unless called together by the President in a special session. We had polled the new Congress by personal interviews and by post and found a safe, two-thirds majority for the amendment in the House. In the new Senate we still lacked a fateful one vote.

Our task was, therefore, to induce the President to call a special session of Congress at the earliest possible moment and to pressure him to obtain the last vote. To that end Alice Paul immediately arranged a demonstration in New York where President Wilson was to address a mass meeting in the Metropolitan Opera House on behalf of his proposed League of Nations before returning to Europe. We planned to hold banners outside the Opera House and to burn his speech at a public meeting nearby.

It was a clear, starry night on March 4, 1919, when the picket line of twenty-five women proceeded with tricolored banners from New York Headquarters to the Opera House. As we neared the corner opposite the Opera House two hundred policemen in close formation rushed us with unbelievable ferocity. They spoke not a word but beat us back with their clubs with such cruelty as none of us had ever witnessed before.

The women clung to their heavy poles, trying to keep the banners flying. But the police seized them, tore the pennants, broke the poles, some of them over our backs, trampled them underfoot, pounded and dragged us. An enormous crowd quickly gathered, made up mostly of soldiers and sailors, many of whom had just returned from abroad and were thronging the streets of New York. They joined forces with the police in the attack.

Margaretta Schuyler, a fragile young girl, was holding a silken American flag which she had carried at the head of the procession when a uniformed soldier jumped upon her, twisted her arms until she cried in pain, cursed, struggled until he had torn her flag from its pole, and then broke the pole across her head.

When I appealed to the policeman, who at that moment was pounding me on the back, to intercept the cruel attack, his only reply was, "Oh, he's helping me." I cried out, "Shame, shame! Aren't you ashamed to beat American women in this brutal way? If we are breaking any law, arrest us! Don't beat us in this cowardly fashion!"

Suffragists attacked on the picket line by an angry mob. (National Woman's Party)

"We'll rush you like bulls," was his vulgar answer. "We've only just begun."

Another young woman was seized by the coat collar and thrown to the pavement for trying to keep hold of her banner. She was trampled under foot and her face severely cut before we could rescue her with the assistance of a sympathetic member of the crowd. There were many shouts of disapproval of the police conduct and many cheers for the women from the crowd.

By this time the crowd was so thick that we could hardly move an inch. It was apparent that we could neither make our way to the Opera House nor could we extricate ourselves. But the terrors continued. Women were knocked down, some of them almost unconscious, others bleeding from the hands and face; arms were bruised and twisted; pocketbooks were snatched and wristwatches stolen.

Six of us were arrested and taken to the police station. One by one we were called to the desk to give our name, age, and various other pieces of information. We stood perfectly silent before the station lieutenant as he coaxed us, "You'd better tell. You'd better give us your name. Tell us where you live—it will make things easier for you." But we continued our silence. We were charged with disorderly conduct, interfering with the police, and assaulting the police. We were locked in separate cells and told we would be taken to the Woman's Night Court for immediate trial. But instead, in about half an hour, we were told we were free to go, that an order had been given by telephone to release us.

We jubilantly left the station house, returning at once to our comrades. There the battle was still going on, and as we joined them we were again dragged and cuffed by the police, but there were no more arrests.

Elsie Hill succeeded in speaking from a balcony above the heads of the crowd. She called out to the soldiers:

> Did you men turn back when you saw the Germans coming? What would you have thought of any one who did? Did you expect us to turn back? We never turn back, either, and we won't until democracy is won! Who rolled bandages for you when you were suffering abroad? Who bound your wounds in your fight

for democracy? Who spent long hours of the night and the day knitting you warm garments? There are women here tonight attempting to hold banners to remind the President that democracy is not won at home, who have given their sons and husbands for your fight abroad. What would they say if they could see you, their comrades in the fight over there, attacking their mothers, their sisters, their wives over here? Aren't you ashamed that you have not enough sporting blood to allow us to make our fight in our own way? Aren't you ashamed that you accepted the help of women in your fight, and now tonight brutally attack them?

And they did listen, until the police in formation—looking like wooden soldiers—advanced from both sides of the street and succeeded in cutting off the crowd from Miss Hill.

The meeting was broken up, and we abandoned any further attempt that night. As our little, bannerless procession filed slowly back to Headquarters, hoodlums followed us. The police gave us no protection and just as we were entering the door of our own building one man struck me on the side of the head with a heavy banner pole. The blow knocked me senseless against the stone building; my hat was snatched from my head and burned in the street. We entered the building to find that soldiers and sailors had broken in during our absence, dragging out bundles of our banners and burning them in the street without any protest from the police.

The next morning, New York newspaper headlines read, "Two hundred maddened women try to see the President;" "Two hundred women attack the police."

It hurt to have the world think we had attacked the police, but that was not important, for the President also read the New York papers as he sailed away to Europe that day. He knew that we were not submitting in silence to his inaction.

CHAPTER TWENTY-SIX

Passage of the Nineteenth Amendment

ALTHOUGH A REPUBLICAN CONGRESS had been elected, President Wilson, as head of the Administration, was still responsible for initiating and guiding legislation. We had to see to it that, with his party out of power, he did not relax his efforts on behalf of the amendment.

To our advantage was the fact that two new Democratic Senators had been elected through the President's influence. He, therefore, had very specific power over these two men, who were neither committed against suffrage by previous votes nor were they yet won to the amendment. One of these men could provide the winning vote. Constant pressure, therefore, was put on the President to win one of these men. When we could see no activity on his part, we threatened publicly to resume dramatic protests against him.

Such a situation gave friends of the Administration considerable alarm. They realized that the slightest attack on the President at that moment would jeopardize his many other worldwide endeavors. A most anxious cable, signed by politicians in his own party, was sent to the President in Paris explaining the serious situation and urging him to do his utmost to secure the vote of one of these Senators at once.

One of the newly elected men, Senator William Harris of Georgia, happened to be in Italy. When he received an unexpected telegram asking him to come to Paris, he journeyed with all speed to the President who asked for his vote on the national suffrage amendment. Senator Harris there and then gave his vote, the sixty-fourth vote.

On that day the passage by Congress of the original Susan B. Anthony amendment was assured.

Immediately a cable was received at the White House carrying news to the suffragists of the final capture of the elusive last vote. A second cable called the new Congress into special session May 19.

The Sixty-sixth Congress convened in Special Session May 19, 1919. Instantly Republican leaders now in control of Congress caucused and organized for a prompt passage of the amendment. On May 21 the Republican House of Representatives passed the measure by a vote of 304 to 89. This was forty-two votes above the required two-thirds majority, whereas the vote in the House in January 1918, under Democratic control, had given the measure only one vote more than was needed.

The Democratic National Committee immediately passed a resolution calling on the legislatures of the various states to hold special legislative sessions, where necessary, to ratify the amendment as soon as it was through Congress in order to "enable women to vote in the national elections of 1920."

When the sixty-fourth vote in the Senate was assured, two more Republicans announced their support, and on June 4 the measure passed the Senate by a vote of 66 to 30—two votes more than needed. Of the forty-nine Republicans in the Senate, forty voted for the amendment, nine against. Of the forty-seven Democrats in the Senate, twenty-six voted for it and twenty-one against.

And so the assertion that "the right of citizens of the United States to vote shall not be denied or abridged by the United States or by any state on account of sex," introduced into Congress by the efforts of Susan B. Anthony in 1878, was finally submitted to the States for ratification on June 4, 1919.

I do not need to explain that the amendment was not won from the Republican Congress between May 19 and June 4, 1919. The Republican Party had been gradually coming to our side throughout our entire national agitation beginning in 1913. And our attack upon the party in power, which happened to be President Wilson's party, had been the most decisive factor in stimulating the opposition party to support our cause. It was perhaps fortunate for the Republican Party that it was their political opponents who inherited this situation in 1913. It was, however, a Republican Congress who promptly and ungrudgingly passed the amendment the moment they came into power. But it will not surprise anyone who has read this book that I conclude by pointing out that the real triumph belongs to the women.

When all suffrage controversy has died away it will be the little army of women with their purple, white and gold banners, going to prison for their political freedom, that will be remembered. They dramatized to victory the long suffrage fight in America. The challenge of the picket line roused the Government out of its half-century sleep of indifference. It stirred the country to hot controversy. It made zealous friends and violent enemies. It produced the sharply drawn contest which forced the surrender of the Government in the second Administration of President Wilson.

Our sole objective was the national enfranchisement of women, the first step in the long struggle of women for political, economic and social emancipation. If political institutions as we know them today break down, and another kind of organization supplants them, women will battle for their place in the new system with as much determination as they have shown in the struggle just ended.

That women have been aroused never again to be content with their subjection there can be no doubt. That they will ultimately secure for themselves equal power and responsibility in whatever system of government is evolved is certain. How revolutionary will be the changes when women get this power and responsibility no one can adequately foretell. One thing is certain. They will not go back. They will never again be good and willing slaves.

As for Alice Paul, she was a master strategist. She abandoned the easy life of a scholar and the aristocratic environment of a cultured, prosperous Quaker family for the rigors of a ceaseless drudgery and frequent imprisonment. Among the thousands of telegrams sent Miss Paul the day the amendment finally passed Congress, was a message from Walter Clark, Chief Justice of the Supreme Court of North Carolina. It read:

Will you permit me to congratulate you upon the great triumph in which you have been so important a factor? Your place in history is assured. Some years ago when I first met you I predicted that your name would be written "on the dusty roll the ages keep." There were politicians, and a large degree of public sentiment, which could only be won by the methods you adopted....
It is certain that, but for you, success would have been delayed for many years to come.

It has been a long, wearying struggle. The relief that comes after a great achievement is sweet. To be sure, women have often resented it deeply that so much human energy had to be expended for so simple a right. But whatever disillusionments they have experienced, they have kept their faith in women, and together we have won political power.

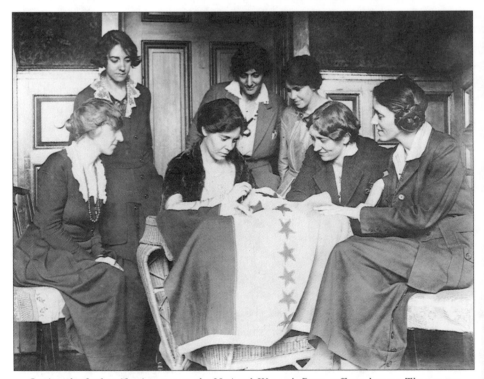

Sewing the final ratification star on the National Woman's Party suffrage banner. The women include (l to r) Mable Vernon, Elizabeth Kalb, Alice Paul, Florence Brewer Boeckel, Anita Pollitzer, Sue White, and Vivian Pearce, 1920. (Schlesinger Library, Radcliffe College)

Afterword

O N J U N E 10, 1919, the state legislature of Wisconsin became the first to ratify the suffrage amendment.

Fourteen months later, on August 18, 1920, Tennessee became the thirty-sixth state to ratify the amendment, providing the necessary three-fourths majority. The ratification by the thirty-sixth and last state legislature proved as difficult to secure as the sixty-fourth and last vote in the United States Senate. But that is a whole other story.

On August 26, 1920, the Secretary of State of the United States proclaimed the Nineteenth Amendment to the Constitution to be the law of the land.

In November 1920, for the first time, all women of the United States were permitted to vote in the national election.

Alice Paul

(1885-1977)

Alice Paul toasting the passage of woman's suffrage, 1920. (National Woman's Party)

The moment Alice Paul first encountered the militant English suffrage movement, securing rights for women became her passion. Her progressive ideas and belief in equality for women had their origin in her well-to-do Quaker family in New Jersey, and after graduating from Swarthmore College in 1905, she became a social worker in New York City. But when she went to England two years later to continue her studies, she instantly felt an affinity for the revolutionary suffrage campaign being waged under the leadership of the Pankhurst women.

The Pankhursts showed Paul that women could never expect to be given the vote; they must take it. For the next three years Paul worked with the Pankhursts. She demonstrated, she went to jail, she was force-fed. These experiences prepared her for the nonviolent militant battle for suffrage she would later wage in her own country.

Back in the United States, it took Paul two years to convince the National American Woman Suffrage Association (NAWSA) to send her to Washington, D. C. to lobby Congress for passage of a federal suffrage amendment. Finally, in December 1912 she arrived in the nation's Capital and set to work. With the help of Lucy Burns and a small group of committed women, Paul organized a spectacular suffrage parade on the day before Woodrow Wilson's inaugural in March 1913. Despite this success, Paul's devotion to militant tactics and her insistence on "holding the party in power responsible" brought her into bitter conflict with the NAWSA, and she soon lost that group's support. She went on to form the National Woman's Party (NWP) in 1916.

Alice Paul was an extraordinary leader, ingenious fundraiser, and brilliant politician. Her entire life revolved around suffrage. She lived in a cold room so she "would not be tempted to sit up late and read novels." Sometimes she went months without bothering to remove her hat. She expected those around her to dedicate themselves totally to suffrage, but she drove no one harder than she drove herself.

After ratification of the Nineteenth Amendment in 1920, Paul earned three law degrees. Then in 1923 at a convention of the National Woman's Party, she proposed the Equal Rights Amendment (ERA), which stipulated that no right shall be denied or abridged by either the federal government or the states on account of sex. She devoted the rest of her life to this new cause. The ERA finally passed Congress in 1972, but it was never ratified by enough states to become part of the Constitution.

Although she failed to secure the Equal Rights Amendment in the United States, Paul achieved a measure of success in the international arena. Largely due to her efforts, women were specifically included in the preamble to the charter of the United Nations, founded after World War II. That document proclaims "the dignity and worth of the human person [and] the equal rights of men and women."

—Carol O'Hare

Lucy Burns
(1879-1966)

Lucy Burns, the major organizer for the National Woman's Party (NWP), was known for her strength of character and fierce determination. Alice Paul praised her as "a thousand times more valiant than I."

A brilliant scholar, Burns at first seemed headed for an outstanding academic career in linguistics. Born in Brooklyn, New York, to an Irish-Catholic family, she graduated from Vassar College and went on to study at Yale, universities in Germany and at Oxford in Cambridge. While in England Burns was exposed to the militant suffrage movement, and in 1909 she gave up her academic pursuits and joined the Women's Social and Political Union, the radical British organization led by the Pankhursts. She spoke out for suffrage on street corners, petitioned Parliament, was arrested, and sent to prison four times. From 1910 to 1912 she campaigned for suffrage in Scotland.

It was in England that Burns first met Alice Paul. In early 1913, after they had both returned to the United States, the two women established the first permanent suffrage headquarters in Washington, D.C., under the auspices of the National American Woman Suffrage Association. They went on to form a highly complementary team similar to that of Elizabeth Cady Stanton and Susan B. Anthony.

As second in command of the Congressional Union and, later, the National Woman's Party, Burns performed a variety of tasks for the cause. She organized the Western campaigns of 1914 and 1916 to defeat Democratic candidates and led most of the NWP picket demonstrations against President Wilson. Lucy Burns was arrested and sentenced to prison six

Lucy Burns (National Woman's Party)

times, proudly serving more time in jail than any other suffragist in America. In November 1917, she went on a nineteen-day hunger strike during which she was forcibly fed.

When the vote was finally won, she refused to take on new battles, including the passage of the Equal Rights Amendment. She abruptly retired from public view and spent the remainder of her life as a conventional, unmarried woman, devoting herself to the Catholic church and to the care of her orphaned niece.

—CAROL O'HARE

Inez Milholland (Boissevain)
(1886-1916)

Inez Milholland, a labor lawyer and a social reformer, was a passionate activist for suffrage. She is also remembered as the beautiful "herald" riding atop a horse, dressed in flowing robes, proudly leading thousands of women in suffrage parades. She carried a golden banner with the words, "Forward Out of Darkness, Forward into Light," which later became the official motto for the National Woman's Party, as well as a slogan used for banners in pickets and parades.

Milholland's suffrage work began as a student at Vassar College where she enrolled two-thirds of her fellow students in a campus suffrage organization.

She went on to earn a law degree at New York University, but her true interest lay in reform causes and she enthusiastically worked for suffrage and the rights of labor. She was a member of several activist organizations, including the Equality League of Self Supporting Women in New York (later the Women's Political Union), the Women's Trade Union League, and the National Association for the Advancement of Colored People.

When the militant Congressional Union was formed by Alice Paul in 1913, Milholland joined. She led the historic March 3, 1913 suffrage parade the day before President Wilson's first inauguration. Later that year she married Eugen Jan Boissevain, and continued her work for woman's suffrage. Tirelessly commit-

Inez Milholland (Library of Congress)

ted, Milholland worked endless hours, traveling long distances. Her passion was evident in her speeches, such as the one she gave at a rally in 1916:

> It is women for women now and shall be until the fight is won! Together we shall stand shoulder to shoulder for the greatest principle the world has known, the right of self-government.
>
> Whatever the party that has ignored the claims of women, we as women must refuse to uphold it. We must refuse to uphold any party until all women are free.
>
> We have nothing but our spirits to rely on and the vitality of our faith, but spirit is invincible.
>
> It is only for a little while. Soon the fight shall be over Victory is in sight.

After several years of constant campaigning for woman's suffrage, Milholland developed pernicious anemia. But despite her ill health, in 1916 she undertook a strenuous speaking tour as part of the NWP's campaign to rally enfranchised women in the Western States to vote against the Democratic Party because of its failure to support a federal suffrage amendment. While speaking in Los Angeles, Milholland collapsed at the podium and died ten weeks later. Hailed as a martyr for the cause, she was memorialized by her suffrage comrades on Christmas day at a service attended by 10,000 people. Milholland became the first woman to be given a memorial service in the nation's Capitol.

—CAROL O'HARE

Alva Smith Belmont
(1853-1933)

Alva Belmont (National Woman's Party)

Alva Smith Vanderbilt Belmont, referred to as Mrs. O.H.P. Belmont in *Jailed for Freedom,* was a woman of vast wealth who gave hundreds of thousands of dollars to the cause of woman suffrage, both in her home state of New York and on the national level.

She acquired much of her large fortune in the divorce granted her in 1895 from William Vanderbilt, grandson of multi-millionaire Cornelius Vanderbilt. As part of the settlement, she received Marble House, their summer home in Newport, Rhode Island, as well as an annual income of $100,000. A year after her divorce she married Oliver Hazard Perry Belmont, son of a prominent banker.

After the death of her husband in 1908, Belmont made a rather unexpected transition from socialite to militant feminist and devoted the rest of her life and much of her money to the causes of working women and woman suffrage. She supported striking garment workers and urged a boycott of nonunion dress manufacturers during the great strikes of 1909. That same year she paid for office space in New York City for the headquarters of the National American Woman Suffrage Association and the Political Equality League, a New York suffrage organization which she founded.

In 1914 Belmont brought Christabel Pankhurst, the English militant suffragist, to the United States and organized her lecture tour. She served on the executive board of the Congressional Union and its successor, the National Woman's Party, from 1914 through 1920. In 1921 she purchased a historic mansion near the Capitol in Washington, D. C. for NWP headquarters and was elected president of that organization.

In explaining her activism, Belmont said that she was convinced that the time had come "to take this world muddle that men have created and…turn it into an ordered, peaceful, happy abiding place for humanity."

—CAROL O'HARE

Maud Younger
(1870-1936)

Maud Younger (National Woman's Party)

During her first thirty years, Maud Younger led the traditional life of an independently wealthy San Francisco socialite. Then, on a whim, she made what she expected to be a brief stop at a settlement house in New York City. When she left five years later, she was an avid believer in suffrage, trade unions, and protective laws for women.

To learn what the life of a working woman was like, she took a job as a waitress and joined the Waitresses' Union. When she returned to San Francisco in 1908, she organized that city's first union for waitresses, becoming known as the "millionaire waitress." She also organized the Wage Earners' Equal Suffrage League for working women and in 1911 helped secure the passage of the woman suffrage amendment to the California State Constitution.

In 1913 Maud Younger joined the Congressional Union where her energy and wide experience made her a valuable asset. A compelling orator, she gave the keynote speech at the founding convention of the National Woman's Party (NWP) in 1916 and the memorial address for Inez Milholland.

The following year she was sent throughout the country to tell the story of the pickets and their treatment in prison. She was also in charge of NWP's committee that lobbied Congress for passage of the federal suffrage amendment. After ratification, she continued her efforts on behalf of working women through the Women's Trade Union League, but from 1923 until her death, she devoted all her efforts to the passage of the Equal Rights Amendment.

—CAROL O'HARE

Rose Winslow

Rose Winslow (Ruza Wenclawska) of New York was a very picturesque figure. Her parents had brought her in infancy from Poland to become a citizen of "free" America. At eleven she was put to work at a loom in a Pennsylvania mill, where she wove hosiery for fourteen hours a day until she contracted tuberculosis at nineteen years of age.

A poet by nature, she developed her mind to the full despite these disadvantages, and when she was forced to abandon her loom, she became an organizer for the Consumers' League, and later the National Woman's Party. Miss Winslow and Alice Paul were the first two suffrag-

Rose Winslow (National Woman's Party)

ists to undertake the hunger strike in prison, and were subjected to forcible feeding. "One feels so forsaken when one lies prone and people shove a pipe down one's stomach," wrote Miss Winslow, describing these feedings in the psychopathic ward. (See Chapter 12.) She was a vivid and eloquent power in the suffrage movement.

—Doris Stevens

Jeannette Rankin
(1880-1973)

In 1916 Jeannette Rankin became the first woman elected to Congress. A lifelong pacifist, she also was the only member of Congress to vote against American entry into both world wars.

Born on a Montana ranch, Rankin graduated from the University of Montana and studied at the New York School of Philanthropy. While a student at the University of Washington, she joined the suffrage campaign that gave women in that state the right to vote in 1910. She went on to lobby full time for suffrage in the Western states, including a successful campaign in her home state of Montana in 1914.

In the 1916 Congressional elections, she ran as a progressive Republican and was elected to the House of Representatives. Only days after taking office in 1917, Rankin voted, along with over fifty men, against entry of the United States into World War I. "I want to stand by my country, but I cannot vote for war," she declared. During the remainder of her term, she sponsored legislation to help women and children and supported a federal suffrage amendment. She was defeated in the next election due largely to her unpopular pacifist stand.

In the years that followed, Rankin was secretary for the National Consumers'

Jeannette Rankin (National Woman's Party)

League and an activist for the Women's International League for Peace and Freedom and other pacifist organizations. In 1940 she again ran for Congress and, on a wave of antiwar sentiment, was elected to a second term in the House of Representatives. In 1941 on the day after Pearl Harbor, Rankin, true to her beliefs and her campaign promises, cast the only vote against entry into World War II. She did not attempt reelection.

Jeannette Rankin continued to work for peace, traveling to India to study Gandhi's methods of nonviolent resistance, opposing involvement in Korea, and actively demonstrating against the Vietnam War.

—CAROL O'HARE

African American Women and Suffrage

Although the Nineteenth Amendment enfranchised *all* women, African American women had to campaign actively to assure their inclusion. They joined the suffrage movement in the 1850s, beginning with Sojourner Truth, and remained throughout the campaign.

As suffrage history is being reclaimed and rewritten, long overdue acknowledgment of African American women's participation is unfolding. Unfortunately, many of their speeches, views, public commentary, and writings either went unrecorded, or were lost to the ages. After emancipation during the post-Civil War years, impoverished Southern black women seeking work, fleeing physical threats to their lives, and struggling with survival strategies for their families, could little afford to make the organized woman suffrage movement a priority. The majority of black women fell into this category, yet, in the formative years from the 1850s through the 1870s, more than 100 African American women have been identified as suffragists. Among them were women such as Harriet Forten Purvis and her sister, Margaretta Forten, who founded the Philadelphia Female Anti-Slavery

Ida B. Wells-Barnett
(University of Chicago)

Society, as well as laying the groundwork for the first National Woman's Rights Convention ever held, in October 1854.

In this early period of suffrage, black women argued that suffrage should be the right of *all* citizens, an argument much like that of white women's suffrage organizations. They based their ideas on classic interpretations of the Constitution and challenged the Fourteenth Amendment, which introduced the word "male" into the Constitution by extending the vote to "Negro males." In this sense, black suffragists' views were quite similar to those of white suffragists such as Elizabeth Cady Stanton and Susan B. Anthony.

The African American woman suffrage argument expanded and developed new rationales from the 1880s until the Nineteenth Amendment was ratified in 1920. During the latter part of the nineteenth century, black women began to view suffrage specifically as a means to benefit black women because they could use the vote to improve their communities and their own lives. As the century turned, greater numbers of black women across the country began to flex their political muscles and demand the right to vote.

Activists included Ida B. Wells-Barnett, who founded the first black woman's suffrage association in the early years of the twentieth century, the Alpha Suffrage Club of Chicago. Its membership marched with white women in suffrage parades. As a journalist and part owner of a newspaper, Wells-Barnett had a strong reputation for writing against lynching, courageously speaking out during the worst of the Jim Crow days in the South.

Many consider Wells-Barnett as virtually unique in her time as a woman who espoused a radical philosophy for racial and gender equality.

The National Association of Colored Women (NACW), a nationwide organization of black women's clubs, also strongly supported suffrage and repeatedly adopted resolutions of cooperation with other suffrage associations. With representation from women's clubs numbering in the thousands, NACW published literature and furnished speakers for the cause. Club women such as Josephine St. Pierre Ruffin, who worked through the NACW, and Mary Church Terrell (the first president of NACW), who picketed the White House with the National Woman's Party, were strong advocates of the suffrage cause. Nannie Helen Burroughs was a distinguished educator whose National Training School for Women and Girls became a model throughout the nation. As an active suffrage promoter, Burroughs published an article in 1915 in the *Crisis,* the magazine of the NAACP, in support of the woman's vote. Articles espousing woman's suffrage appeared not only in black women's club newsletters and journals, but also in mainstream black periodicals.

However, black women continued to suffer discrimination against their efforts to participate in the political process and to join in the struggle to gain the vote for women. There were attempts, primarily by Southerners, to insert the words "white only" in the Susan B. Anthony suffrage amendment, as well as attempts to have substitute amendments that excluded black women. There were also strategies introduced by white women suffragists in the South to "sell" woman suffrage to Southern Congressmen and to gain their support by demonstrating that white women in the South would potentially outnumber—therefore out vote—*all* blacks in the South. Their plea for enfranchising women would be a strategy to maintain white supremacy.

Despite discrimination against black women by many white women in both the mainstream and militant suffrage organizations, African American women remained actively engaged in suffrage. Significantly, black suffragists began to distinguish their problems from those of white women and from those of black men, realizing that the vote would help them better their situation in society, facing both sexism and racism.

After the passage of the Nineteenth Amendment, many African Americans—both men and women—continued to be denied the vote through a series of state exclusionary measures. However, the guarantee of this right in the Constitution afforded African Americans another weapon in their fight for racial and political equality throughout the remainder of the twentieth century.

— ROSALYN TERBORG-PENN
Professor of History, Morgan State University

English Militant Suffrage Movement

In 1903 Emmeline Pankhurst and her daughters Christabel and Sylvia founded the Women's Social and Political Union (WSPU) in England. Its objective was to be independent of any political party and to persuade the public to vote against any parliamentary candidate who did not support votes for women. Although other woman suffrage organizations had long existed, the WSPU was the first and largest militant group. It drew much of its early support from working women.

The suffragettes, as they were called, sought new methods to achieve political equality: demonstration, confrontation and peaceful agitation at first and, later, more radical tactics. When the women were arrested for their activities, they chose prison over paying fines, went on hunger strikes and endured forced feeding. They suffered appalling physical hardship, beatings, and other brutal treatment. Over one thousand members of the WSPU were eventually imprisoned. Emmeline Pankhurst nearly died from numerous hunger strikes.

Describing her deep commitment to votes for women, Emmeline Pankhurst wrote:

> I had been reared in the suffrage cause and the principle of equality had been lived out in our home. In fact it was the sharp contrast between practical suffragism in the home circle and the inequality I saw meted out to women in general in the outer world that made me see in the suffrage cause one, not of merely academic interest, but of stern practical importance.
>
> Here, then, was an aim in life for me—the liberation of politically fettered womanhood.
>
> One decision I came to firmly; it was that this vote question must be settled. Mine was the third generation of women to claim the vote and the vote must now be obtained. To go on helplessly pleading was undignified. Strong and urgent demand was needed. Success must be hastened or women's last political state would be worse than their first.

The WSPU's challenge to the government lasted until 1914 when England became involved in World War I. Partial suffrage was granted to women in 1918; universal women's suffrage came ten years later.

—CAROL O'HARE

National American Woman Suffrage Association

In 1890 two rival suffrage organizations, one headed by Susan B. Anthony and Elizabeth Cady Stanton and the other by Lucy Stone and Julia Ward Howe, united to form the National American Woman Suffrage Association (NAWSA). By the time Carrie Chapman Catt was made president in 1916, NAWSA had forty-four state auxiliaries with a total membership

Carrie Chapman Catt (Library of Congress)

of more than two million, but it lacked direction and effective organization.

Carrie Chapman Catt went on to become the most powerful political leader of the woman's rights movement. Although her real goal was the passage of a federal suffrage amendment, she believed Congress would not act until women were able to vote in national elections in enough states to make ratification a possibility. She thus devised her "Winning Plan," which promoted work in state suffrage campaigns while simultaneously lobbying for the federal amendment.

The National American Woman Suffrage Association used very different tactics from Alice Paul and the National Woman's Party. While the NWP engaged in dramatic, militant action, NAWSA chose gentle persuasion and respectable campaigning. Both methods would prove necessary in the eventual achievement of the women's suffrage amendment, its passage by Congress, and ratification by the states.

In 1920 NAWSA became the League of Women Voters and dedicated itself to local civic matters, to the education of newly enfranchised women, and to the study of national legislation and social policy.

—CAROL O'HARE

Suffrage in the Western States

Wyoming was the first state to grant women the right to vote when it became a state in 1890. (As a territory, women in Wyoming had won that right in

Pickets released from jail demand new court hearing for the imprisoned Alice Paul.
(National Woman's Party)

1869.) By the time Alice Paul went to Washington, D.C. in 1913, women could vote in nine states, all in the West: Wyoming (1890); Colorado (1893); Utah (1895); Idaho (1896); Washington (1910); California (1911); Oregon, Arizona, and Kansas (1912). Western states, because of their liberal frontier tradition, were more likely to grant women freedom and political rights.

Women in these nine Western states could vote in all elections—local, state and national. They could cast a vote in presidential elections while women who lived in other states could not.

In 1913 Illinois became the first state east of the Mississippi to permit women suffrage, although it was limited to municipal and presidential elections. Nevada and Montana were added in 1914.

—CAROL O'HARE

Illegal Arrests

In August 1917, when it was clear that the policy of imprisoning suffragists would be continued indefinitely and under longer sentences, the next three groups of pickets to be arrested asked for a decision from the District Court of Appeals. Justice Charles H. Robb, after granting two appeals, refused to grant any more, upon the ground that he had discretionary power to grant or withhold an appeal. When further right of appeal was denied us, and when the Administration persisted in arresting us, we were compelled either to stop picketing or to go to prison.

The first appealed case was heard by the Court of Appeals on January 8, 1918, and the decision handed down in favor of the defendants on March 4, 1918. This decision was concurred in by all three judges.

In effect, the decisions declared that every one of the 218 suffragists arrested up to that time had been arrested illegally. Those who had been found guilty had been convicted illegally, and the ninety-seven who went to jail had been illegally imprisoned. The whole policy of the Administration in arresting women was thus shown to be lawless. The women could, if they had chosen, have filed suits for damages for false arrest and imprisonment.

The appeal cases of the other pickets were ordered dismissed and stricken from the records.

— Doris Stevens

The Equal Rights Amendment

When the Nineteenth Amendment granted women the right to vote in 1920, many suffrage leaders thought women finally had entered the mainstream of political life. Others knew, however, that while the vote was crucial, it did not change the fact that the law often treated women differently from men; laws were gender biased and discriminatory. Getting the vote was an important first step but the work of gaining equality was not over. Just as the abolitionists recognized that the Thirteenth Amendment's end to slavery was not sufficient for ensuring civil rights for former slaves and so added the Fourteenth and Fifteenth Amendments to guarantee specific rights, the suffragists also understood that the best way to guarantee equal rights for women was through another constitutional amendment.

In 1923, Alice Paul and the leaders of the National Woman's Party (NWP), the radicals of the suffrage movement, held a convention to discuss state laws that discriminated against women. For instance, women could not be on juries, they did not receive the same pay as men for the same work, they could not inherit or will their property the same as men, they were barred from certain jobs to "protect" them and, if they married a man from a foreign country, they lost their American citizenship. The NWP convention proposed the Equal Rights Amendment to the Constitution, and it was introduced into Congress in 1923 by Representative Daniel Anthony of Kansas, Susan B. Anthony's nephew.

In 1923, the proposed ERA stated:

> Men and women shall have equal rights throughout the United States and every place subject to its jurisdiction. Congress shall have the power to enforce this article by appropriate legislation.

The wording was later changed in 1943 to conform legally to the format of the other constitutional amendments. The new version stated:

> Equality of Rights under the law shall not be denied or abridged by the United States or by any State on account of sex.

For numerous reasons, the ERA began a bitter controversy and debate in the women's movement that has lasted to the present. The National Woman's Party pointed out that "protective" laws often kept women from getting higher paid jobs and created an unfair advantage for men.

However, the National American Woman Suffrage Association (NAWSA), the mainstream suffrage group, which became the League of Women Voters in 1920, along with many other women's groups had worked for more than thirty years to pass laws that protected women from harsh labor conditions. They were concerned that the ERA would rescind their hard-won battles for key employment laws such as minimum wage and maximum hours laws. This dispute caused a split that damaged the women's movement and was not healed until the contemporary women's movement in the early 1970s.

Because women were divided, and since there was little public outcry for women to have equal legal rights with men, the ERA made little progress from 1923 until the early 1970s. Introduced in every session of Congress during that time, the ERA was never debated by Congress. In the late 1960s, a new women's movement had become active and the ERA was revived. There was great public support for women to have equal access with men to all aspects of American life: education, the military, sports, salaries, and the professions. Women's groups believed that they could now rally enough congressional votes to get the ERA passed by Congress.

In March 1972, Congress passed the ERA and sent it to the states to be ratified. Activist women's groups such as the National Organization for Women, the Women's Political Caucus, the League of Women Voters, and many others worked vigorously to pass the ERA. By the end of 1973, thirty-one states had ratified the amendment, but ratification by thirty-eight states was required.

Soon after the initial wave of enthusiasm for the ERA, opponents began to organize and to build momentum for the amendment's defeat. People were often confused by what the amendment meant and what it would do. At the time, one of the most damaging arguments against the ERA was that women would be equally eligible to the military draft. (The general public was not aware that Congress already had the right to draft women into the military with the Nurses Selective Service Bill of 1945.) In addition, some feared it would end women's role in the home, destroy the family, force men and women to use the same bathrooms, and permit husbands not to support their wives. The fight for passage of the ERA grew even more heated and confusing when abortion rights entered the debate after the Supreme Court's decision in 1973 in *Roe v. Wade.*

Those against the ERA were led by conservative political, business, and religious organizations who saw this cause as a highly effective rallying tool. The public spokeswoman heading the fight against the ERA was conservative Republican Phyllis Schlafley who said that women had the best of all possible worlds already and should not "stoop to equality."

Both sides waged strong campaigns. Congress had set a deadline of 1977 by which the proposed amendment must be ratified or it would expire. When not enough states ratified the ERA by 1977, supporters lobbied, petitioned, and staged parades and demonstrations successfully extending the deadline to pass the ERA to 1982. By the end, opponents of the ERA were more successful in frightening the public about the supposed destruction of the family and the end of women's role in the home than its supporters were in convincing the public of the ERA's benefit. The amendment failed to be ratified by the needed number of states and the deadline for ratification expired in 1982.

Since then, the ERA has been re-introduced in Congress but has not gained enough votes to pass. Women's groups have since sought other ways to gain equality for women—through equal pay for equal work, enforcing existing laws on equal education and access to jobs, by nominating more women for political office, and by entering the professions in unprecedented numbers. Women are still divided over the need for the ERA, but continue to seek equal protection under the law.

—Edith Mayo

Alice Paul (second from right) and National Woman's Party members displaying their banner with a Susan B. Anthony quote. (Library of Congress)

Countries in Which Women Vote

Compiled by Doris Stevens, 1920

Azerbijain		Iceland	1919
(Moslem) Republic	1919	Ireland	1918
Australia	1902	Isle of Man	1881
Austria	1918	Luxembourg	1919
Belgium[1]	1919	Mexico[3]	1917
British East Africa	1919	New Zealand	1893
Canada	1918	Norway	1907
Czecho Slovakia	1918	Poland	1918
Denmark	1915	Rhodesia	1919
England[2]	1918	Russia	1917
Finland	1906	Scotland	1918
Germany	1918	Sweden[4]	1919
Holland	1919	United States	1920
Hungary	1918	Wales	1918

1. Electoral Reform Bill as passed granted suffrage to widows who have not remarried and mothers of soldiers killed in battle or civilians shot by Germans.

2. Women over age of thirty—bill to reduce age to twenty-one has passed its second reading.

3. No sex qualification for voting in constitution. Women have so far not availed themselves of their right to vote, but are expected to do so in the coming elections.

4. To be confirmed in 1920.

Only those who actually served prison sentences are listed below, although more than five hundred women were arrested during picketing and demonstrations in Washington, DC and Boston. This list was compiled by Doris Stevens in 1920.

MINNIE D. ABBOTT, Atlantic City, NJ. Officer National Woman's Party (NWP).

MRS. PAULINE ADAMS, Norfolk, VA, wife of physician.

EDITH AINGE, Jamestown, NY, native of England.

HARRIET U. ANDREWS, Kansas City, MO, war worker.

MRS. ANNIE ARNEIL, Wilmington, DE. One of first six suffrage prisoners.

BERTHE ARNOLD, Colorado Springs, CO, member of Daughters of the American Revolution (DAR), kindergarten teacher.

VIRGINIA ARNOLD, NC, teacher. Organizer and executive secretary NWP, one of first six pickets arrested and sent to prison.

MRS. W. D. ASCOUGH, Detroit, MI, abandoned concert stage for suffrage work.

MRS. ABBY SCOTT BAKER, Washington, DC, wife of physician, three sons served in World War. Executive committee NWP.

MRS. CHARLES W. BARNES, Indianapolis, IN.

MRS. NAOMI BARRETT, Wilmington, DE.

MRS. W. J. BARTLETT, Putnam, CT, leader of CT state grange.

MRS. M. TOSCAN BENNETT, Hartford, CT, wife of lawyer, member DAR. National Advisory Council NWP.

HILDA BLUMBERG, New York, NY, native of Russia, teacher.

MRS. KATE BOECKH, Washington, DC, native of Canada, one of first women airplane pilots.

MRS. CATHERINE BOYLE, Newcastle, DE, munitions worker during war.

LUCY G. BRANHAM, Baltimore, MD, PhD Columbia University. Organizer NWP.

MRS. LUCY G. BRANHAM, Baltimore, MD, mother of Miss Lucy Branham.

MRS. JOHN WINTERS BRANNAN, New York, NY, wife of physician. Executive committee NWP, officer Woman's Political Union in NY.

JENNIE BRONENBERG, Philadelphia, PA, student.

MRS. MARY E. BROWN, Wilmington, DE.

LOUISE BRYANT, New York, NY, formerly Portland, OR, author, poet, journalist.

LUCY BURNS, New York, NY, active in English suffrage movement. Vice chairman and member of executive committee of Congressional Union for Woman Suffrage and NWP, leader of most picket demonstrations, served more time in jail than any other suffragist in America.

MRS. HENRY BUTTERWORTH, New York, NY, active in civic and suffrage work in NY.

IRIS CALDERHEAD, Marysville, KS, daughter of former Congressman, teacher. Organizer NWP.

MRS. LUCILLE A. CALMES, Princeton, IA, government worker during war.

ELEANOR CALNAN, Methuen, MA.

MRS. AGNES CHASE, Washington, DC, formerly of IL, engaged in scientific research for US Department of Agriculture.

MRS. PALYS L. CHEVRIER, New York, NY. Member "Prison Special."

MRS. HELEN CHISASKI, Bridgeport, CT, munitions worker and member of Machinists' Union.

MRS. WILLIAM CHISHOLM, Huntington, PA.

JOSEPHINE COLLINS, Framingham, MA, store owner. One of first members of NWP.

MRS. SARAH TARLETON COLVIN, St. Paul, MN, wife of physician, Red Cross nurse. MN state chairman NWP, member "Prison Special."

BETTY CONNOLLY, West Newton, MA, household assistant.

MRS. ALICE M. COSU, New Orleans, LA. Vice chairman LA state NWP.

CORA CRAWFORD, Philadelphia, PA, business woman.

GERTRUDE CROCKER, Washington, DC, formerly of IL, government worker. Treasurer NWP.

RUTH CROCKER, Washington, DC, formerly of IL, sister of Gertrude Crocker.

MRS. L. J. C. DANIELS, Grafton, VT, and Boston.

DOROTHY DAY, New York, NY, journalist, member Socialist Party and Industrial Workers of the World.

EDNA DIXON, Washington, DC, public school teacher.

LAVINIA I. DOCK, Fayetteville, PA, secretary American Federation of Nurses, author of nursing textbooks, founder of visiting nurse movement in New York. One of first six pickets arrested and sent to prison.

MRS. MARY CARROLL DOWELL, Philadelphia, PA, wife of magazine editor. Officer PA state NWP.

MARY DUBROW, Passaic, NJ, teacher.

JULIA EMORY, Baltimore, MD, daughter of state senator, worker for Trade Union League.

MRS. EDMUND C. EVANS, Ardmore, PA, one of three Winsor sisters who served prison terms.

LUCY EWING, Chicago, IL, daughter of judge, niece of US vice president under Cleveland. Officer IL state NWP.

MRS. ESTELLA EYLWARD, New Orleans, LA, business woman.

MARY GERTRUDE FENDALL, Baltimore, MD. Treasurer NWP.

ELLA FINDEISEN, Lawrence, MA.

KATHARINE FISHER, Washington, DC, native of MA, teacher, social worker, feminist writer.

MRS. ROSE GRATZ FISHSTEIN, Philadelphia, PA, native of Russia, factory worker, union organizer.

ROSE FISHSTEIN, Philadelphia, PA, sister-in-law of Mrs. Rose G. Fishstein, native of Russia, business woman.

CATHERINE M. FLANAGAN, Hartford, CT, daughter of Irish exile. Organizer NWP.

MARTHA FOLEY, Dorchester, MA, active in labor movement.

MRS. T. W. FORBES, Baltimore, MD.

JANET FOTHERINGHAM, Buffalo, NY, teacher of physical education.

MARGARET FOTHERINGHAM, Buffalo, NY, dietician.

FRANCES FOWLER, Brookline, MA.

MRS. MATILDA HALL GARDNER, Washington, DC, formerly of Chicago, wife of newspaper journalist. Executive committee NWP.

ANNA GINSBERG, New York, NY.

REBA GOMBOROV, Philadelphia, PA, native of Russia, social worker, president Office Workers' Association, member Trade Union League.

ALICE GRAM, Portland, OR.

BETTY GRAM, Portland, OR, abandoned stage career for suffrage work.

NATALIE GRAY, Colorado Springs, CO, daughter of officer CO state NWP.

MRS. FRANCIS GREEN, New York, NY.

GLADYS GREINER, Baltimore, MD, settlement worker in KY mountains, tennis and golf champion.

MRS. J. IRVING GROSS, Boston, MA. Charter member MA state NWP.

ANNA GWINTER, New York, NY.

ELIZABETH HAMILTON, New York, NY.

ERNESTINE HARA, New York, NY, native of Romania.

REBECCA HARRISON, Joplin, MO.

MRS. H. O. HAVEMEYER (Louisine Waldron), New York, NY, generous contributor to suffrage causes. Member "Prison Special."

KATE HEFFELFINGER, Shamokin, PA, art student.

MRS. JESSICA HENDERSON, Boston, MA, mother of six, daughter also arrested.

MINNIE HENNESY, Hartford, CT, business woman.

ANNE HERKIMER, Baltimore, MD, child labor inspector.

ELSIE HILL, Norwalk, CT, daughter of former Congressman, French teacher. Executive committee Congressional Union, organizer NWP.

MRS. GEORGE HILL, Boston, MA.

MRS. FLORENCE BAYARD HILLES, Newcastle, DE, daugher of former ambassador to Britain and secretary of state, munitions worker during war. Executive committee NWP.

MRS. J. A. H. HOPKINS (Allison Turnbull), Morristown, NJ, wife of member of Wilson's Democratic National Campaign Committee.

MRS. L. H. HORNBY, New York, NY, formerly of IL, one of first women aviators in US.

ELIZABETH HUFF, Des Moines, IA, worked for war department.

EUNICE HUFF, Des Moines, IA, sister of Elizabeth.

HAZEL HUNKINS, Billings, MT, university chemistry instructor. Organizer NWP.

JULIA HURLBUT, Morristown, NJ, engaged in war work in France. Vice chairman NJ state NWP.

MARY INGHAM, Philadelphia, PA, active in Women's Trade Union League, investment broker. Chairman PA state NWP.

MRS. MARK JACKSON, Baltimore, MD.

PAULA JAKOBI, New York, NY, playwright.

MAUD JAMISON, Norfolk, VA, high school teacher and business woman. One of first six pickets arrested and sent to prison.

MRS. PEGGY BAIRD JOHNS, New York, NY, formerly of St. Louis, newspaper and magazine writer.

WILLIE GRACE JOHNSON, Shreveport, LA, business woman. Officer LA state NWP.

AMY JUENGLING, Buffalo, NY.

ELIZABETH GREEN KALB, Houston, TX. Head of NWP library.

RHODA KELLOGG, Minneapolis, MN.

MRS. FREDERICK W. KENDALL (Ada Davenport), Hamburg, NY, wife of newspaper editor, writer and public speaker.

MARIE ERNST KENNEDY, Philadelphia, PA. Chairman PA state NWP.

Mrs. Margaret Wood Kessler, Denver, CO.

Alice Kimball, New York, NY, librarian, labor investigator.

Mrs. Beatrice Kinkead, Montclair, NJ.

Mrs. Ruby E. Koenig, Hartford, CT.

Hattie Kruger, Buffalo, NY, nurse, probation officer, ran for Congress on Socialist ticket in 1918.

Dr. Anna Kuhn, Baltimore, MD, physician.

Mrs. Lawrence Lewis (Dora), Philadelphia, PA, family ancestors came to America in 1660. Treasurer and member executive committee NWP

Katherine Lincoln, New York, NY, formerly of Philadelphia.

Dr. Sarah H. Lockrey, Philadelphia, PA, surgeon.

Elizabeth McShane, Philadelphia, PA, school principal, business woman.

Mrs. Agnes J. Magee, Wilmington, DE.

Mrs. Effie B. Main, Topeka, KS.

Maud Malone, New York, NY, librarian, lifelong suffragist.

Anne Martin, Reno, NV, professor of history, ran for US Senate as independent in 1918. Led successful fight for NV suffrage 1914, vice chairman NWP.

Mrs. Louise Parker Mayo, Framingham, MA, mother of seven.

Nell Mercer, Norfolk, VA, business woman.

Vida Milholland, New York, NY, sister of Inez Milholland (Boissevain), gave up singing career for suffrage work.

Mrs. Bertha Moller, Minneapolis, MN, family came from Sweden.

Martha W. Moore, Philadelphia, PA, engaged in social service work. Charter member Congressional Union.

Mrs. Agnes H. Morey, Brookline, MA, colonial ancestry. Founder and chairman MA state NWP, National Advisory Council NWP.

Katherine A. Morey, Brookline, MA, daughter of Mrs. A. H. Morey. Officer MA state NWP, one of first six pickets arrested and sent to prison.

Mildred Morris, Denver, CO, newspaper woman.

Mrs. Phoebe C. Munnecke, Detroit, MI.

Gertrude Murphy, Minneapolis, MN, public school superintendent of music.

Mrs. Mary A. Nolan, Jacksonville, FL, member of Confederate organizations. Suffrage pioneer, oldest suffrage prisoner.

Mrs. Margaret Oakes, ID.

Alice Paul, Morristown, NJ, PhD, active in English suffrage movement.

Founder and chairman Congressional Union for Woman Suffrage, founder and chairman National Woman's Party. While in jail, suffered severest treatment of any suffrage prisoner.

BERRY POTTIER, Boston, MA, art student.

EDNA M. PARTELL, Hartford, CT.

MRS. R. B. QUAY, Salt Lake City, UT.

MRS. BETSY REYNEAU, Detroit, MI, wife of portrait painter.

MRS. C. T. ROBERTSON, Salt Lake City, UT, active in reform movement.

MRS. GEORGE E. ROEWER, Belmont, MA, wife of attorney.

MRS. JOHN ROGERS, Jr, New York, NY, wife of physician, descendent of signer of Declaration of Independence. Chairman National Advisory Council NWP, member of "Suffrage Special" and "Prison Special."

MARGUERITE ROSSETTE, Baltimore, MD, artist.

MRS. ELISE T. RUSSIAN, Detroit, MI, born in Constantinople, teacher. Officer MI state NWP.

NINA SAMARODIN, native of Russia, union organizer.

MRS. PHOEBE PERSONS SCOTT, Morristown, NJ, worked at settlement house. Officer NWP.

RUTH SCOTT, Bridgeport, CT, munitions worker.

BELLE SHEINBERG, New York, NY, student.

MRS. LUCILLE SHIELDS, Amarillo, TX.

MRS. MARTHA REED SHOEMAKER, Philadelphia, PA.

MRS. MARY SHORT, Minneapolis, MN. Officer MN state NWP.

MRS. LOIS WARREN SHAW, Manchester, NH, mother of six. Chairman NH state NWP.

RUTH SMALL, Boston, MA.

DR. CAROLINE E. SPENCER, Colorado Springs, CO, formerly of Philadelphia, physician. Secretary CO state NWP.

MRS. KATE STAFFORD, Oklahoma City, OK, reform worker, mother of six.

DORIS STEVENS, Omaha, NE, social worker, teacher. Organized first convention of women voters in 1915. Officer and member executive committee NWP. (See also page 214.)

ELIZABETH STUYVESANT, New York, NY, formerly of Cincinnati, dancer, active in birth control reform.

ELSIE UNTERMAN, Chicago, IL, social worker.

MABEL VERNON, Wilmington, DE, high school teacher. Organizer and secretary NWP, one of first six pickets arrested and sent to prison.

MRS. ELSIE VERVANE, Bridgeport, CT, munitions worker, union activist.

MRS. ROBERT WALKER, Baltimore, MD. Officer MD state NWP.

BERTHA WALLERSTEIN, New York, NY, student.

MRS. BERTHA WALMSLEY, Kansas City, MO, government worker.

MRS. WILLIAM UPTON WATSON, Chicago, IL. Treasurer IL state NWP.

MRS. C. WEAVER, Bridgeport, CT, munitions worker.

EVA WEAVER, Bridgeport, CT, daughter of Mrs. C. Weaver, also munitions worker.

MRS. HELENA HILL WEED, Norwalk, CT, daughter of former Congressman, member DAR, geologist.

CORA A. WEEK, New York, NY, artist.

CAMILLA WHITCOMB, Worcester, MA.

SUE WHITE, Jackson, TN, descendent of prominent pioneer families, court reporter. Chairman TN state NWP, editor of NWP publication, *The Suffragist*.

MARGARET FAY WHITTEMORE, Detroit, MI, daughter of patent attorney. Organizer NWP.

MRS. HARVEY W. WILEY, Washington, DC, wife of former director of government pure food department. National Advisory Council NWP.

ROSE WINSLOW, New York, NY, native of Poland, factory worker.

MARY WINSOR, Haverford, PA. Member of "Prison Special."

ELLEN WINSOR, Haverford, PA, sister of Mary Winsor and Mrs. Edmund C. Evans, who also served prison terms.

MRS. KATE WINSTON, Chevy Chase, MD, wife of professor.

CLARA WOLD, Portland, OR, newspaper writer.

JOY YOUNG, New York, NY, formerly of Washington, DC. Organizer NWP.

MATILDA YOUNG, Washington, DC, sister of Joy Young. Youngest picket arrested (age 19).

Suggested Readings

Books

Kathleen Barry, *Susan B. Anthony: A Biography of a Singular Feminist* (New York: New York Univ. Press, 1988).

Mari Jo and Paul Buhle, *The Concise History of Woman Suffrage* (Chicago: Univ. of Illinois Press, 1978).

Carrie Chapman Catt, *Woman Suffrage and Politics* (New York: Charles Scribner's Sons, 1923; and Seattle: Univ. of Washington Press, American Library Paperback edition, 1970).

William Chafe, *The American Woman: Her Changing Social, Economic, and Political Role, 1920-1970* (Oxford Univ. Press, 1972).

William Chafe, *Women and Equality: Changing Patterns in American Culture* (Oxford Univ. Press, 1977).

Ellen DuBois, *Feminism and Suffrage: The Emergence of an Independent Women's Movement in America, 1848-1969* (Ithaca: Cornell Univ. Press, 1978).

Eleanor Flexner, *Century of Struggle: The Woman's Rights Movement in the United States* (Cambridge, Massachusetts: Belknap Press of Harvard University Press, 1959; and New York: Atheneum, 1972).

Elisabeth Griffith, *In Her Own Right: The Life of Elizabeth Cady Stanton* (New York: Oxford Univ. Press, 1984).

Allan P. Grimes, *The Puritan Ethic and Woman Suffrage* (Oxford Univ. Press, 1967).

Miriam Gurko, *The Ladies of Seneca Falls* (New York: Macmillan Publishing Co., 1974).

Inez Haynes Irwin, *The Story of Alice Paul and the National Woman's Party* (Fairfax, Virginia: Denlinger's Publishers, 1920, 1964, 1977).

Aileen Kraditor, *Ideas of the Woman Suffrage Movement, 1890-1920* (New York: Columbia Univ. Press, 1965).

J. Stanley Lemons, *The Woman Citizen: Social Feminism in the 1920s.* (Chicago: Univ. of Illinois Press, 1975).

Keith Melder, *Beginnings of Sisterhood: The American Woman's Rights Movement, 1800-1850* (New York: Schocken Books, 1977).

David Morgan, *Suffragists and Democrats: The Politics of Woman Suffrage in America* (East Lansing: Michigan State Univ. Press, 1972).

William L. O'Neill, *Everybody Was Brave* (Chicago: Quadrangle Books, 1969).

Elizabeth Cady Stanton, *Eighty Years and More* (New York: Schocken Books, 1971).

Marjorie Spruill Wheeler, editor, *One Woman One Vote: Rediscovering Woman's Suffrage Movement* (Troutdale, Oregon: NewSage Press, 1995).

ARTICLES

Paula Baker, "The Domestication of Politics: Women and American Political society, 1780-1920," *American Historical Review,* 89 (June 1984), 620-647.

Nancy Cott, "What's in a Name? The Limits of 'Social Feminism,'" *The Journal of American History,* 76:3 (December 1989), 809-829.

Nancy Cott, "Feminist Politics in the 1920s: The National Woman's Party," *The Journal of American History,* 71:1 (June 1984), 43-68.

Ellen Carol DuBois, "Working Women, Class Relations, and Suffrage Militance: Harriot Stanton Blatch and the New York Woman Suffrage Movement," *The Journal of American History,* 74:1 (June 1987), 34-58.

Leila J. Rupp, "Feminism and the Sexual Revolution in the Early Twentieth Century: The Case of Doris Stevens," *Feminist Studies,* 15:2 (Spring 1989), 289-309.

Doris Stevens
(1888-1963)

Doris Stevens (1888-1963) was an ardent, lifelong feminist. Born in Omaha, Nebraska, she graduated from Oberlin College in 1911, already active in suffrage work. After teaching high school for two years, she became a full-time organizer for the Congressional Union for Woman Suffrage in Washington, D.C.

Stevens worked closely with Alice Paul and, after the National Woman's Party (NWP) was formed, became one of its leaders. In 1915, at the Panama Pacific Exposition in San Francisco, she organized the first convention of women voters.

Doris Stevens (Schlesinger Library)

The following year she managed the NWP's election campaign in California. She served the NWP in a variety of capacities: organizer, executive secretary, legislative chair, political chair, and executive committee member. In addition, she was personal companion and assistant to Alva Belmont, NWP's wealthy benefactor.

Stevens was arrested for picketing the White House in June 1917 and sentenced to sixty days in Occoquan workhouse. She served three days before receiving a presidential pardon. She was also arrested at a New York City demonstration but was not sentenced.

In 1921 Stevens married Dudley Field Malone, the attorney who had served as counsel for the NWP. After she divorced him, she married Jonathan Mitchell, a journalist, in 1935. Throughout her marriages, she kept her own name and continued her feminist activities. She ran a Women for Congress campaign in 1924, worked for women's equality in the League of Nations, and became the first chairperson of the Inter-American Commission of Women, a position she held until 1938.

Stevens broke with the NWP in 1947 after litigation over a bequest from the estate of Mrs. Belmont and a bitter lawsuit over party leadership and resources.

She then devoted her energy to the Lucy Stone League, a feminist group in New York. In the 1950s her politics turned to the right; she and her husband supported the anti-communist campaign of Senator Joseph McCarthy.

In the last years of her life, Stevens worked to establish a Lucy Stone Chair of Feminism at Radcliffe College, believing that feminism should be a recognized academic field of study. Her efforts to this end continued even after her death in 1963; in 1986 the Doris Stevens Foundation endowed a chair in women's studies at Princeton University.

Carol O'Hare

Carol O'Hare, editor of this revised edition of *Jailed for Freedom,* has an avid interest in history, especially that pertaining to women. In 1991, she edited and published *How I Learned to Ride the Bicycle: Reflections of an Influential 19th Century Woman* by Frances Willard, resurrecting a century-old classic. She has also authored books on San Francisco Bay Area history and written articles on a variety of topics.

A native of Minneapolis, O'Hare has degrees from the University of Minnesota and Boston University. She has worked as a publisher, editor, health educator, and counselor. She presently resides in Sunnyvale, California.

Edith Mayo

Edith Mayo wrote the new introduction to this edition of *Jailed for Freedom.* She is a curator in the Division of Political History, National Museum of American History, and has been a historian at the Smithsonian Institution for more than twenty years. She received a Master's degree in American Studies from George Washington University.

Since joining the museum's staff, Mayo has curated several major exhibitions on political history, the history of voting rights, and women's history. She developed the Smithsonian's first ladies exhibition to reflect their political and historical importance in the context of presidential and women's history.

In 1990, Mayo curated the permanent exhibition "From Parlor to Politics: Women and Reform in America, 1890-1925," exploring women's entry into reform and politics at the turn of the century and its impact on American social policy. Mayo has also been closely involved in collecting for the museum's holdings in women's history, politics, civil rights, and voting rights. She has written, edited, and contributed to numerous articles and books.

Index

Other Books by NewSage Press

One Woman One Vote
edited by Marjorie Spruill Wheeler

Animals as Teachers and Healers
by Susan Chernak McElroy

Women & Work: In Their Own Words
edited by Maureen R. Michelson

Blue Moon Over Thurman Street
by Ursula K. Le Guin and Roger Dorband

The C-Word: Teenagers and Their Families Living with Cancer
by Elena Dorfman

When the Bough Breaks: Pregnancy and the Legacy of Addiction
by Kira Corser and Frances Payne Adler

A Portrait of American Mothers & Daughters
by Raisa Fastman

Organizing for Our Lives: New Voices from Rural Communities
by Richard Steven Street and Samuel Orozco, Foreword by Cesar Chavez

Family Portraits in Changing Times
by Helen Nestor

Stories of Adoption: Loss & Reunion
by Eric Blau

Common Heroes: Facing a Life Threatening Illness
by Eric Blau

The New Americans: Immigrant Life in Southern California
by Ulli Steltzer

For a NewSage Press Catalog, write or call:

NewSage Press, P.O. Box 607, Troutdale, OR 97060
Phone: 503-695-2211, Fax: 503-695-5406